GENDER, WORK AND POVERTY

SIDDHARTHA SARKAR

SERIALS PUBLICATIONS
NEW DELHI

First Published - 2007

ISBN : 81-8387-076-7

Published by

SERIALS PUBLICATIONS
4830/24, Prahlad Street, Ansari Road
Darya Ganj, New Delhi-110002 (India)
Phone : +91-11-23245225. Fax : +91-11-23272135
E-mail: serials@satyam.net.in

Contents

Prologue

Women in general relative to men face unequal hiring standards, unequal opportunities for training, unequal pay for equal work, unequal access to productive resources, segregation and concentration in female sectors and occupations, different physical and mental working conditions, unequal participation in economic decision-making and unequal promotion prospects. These factors negatively affect women's social status and their position in society relative to men, and consequently have an impact on gender inequalities in health. Women's work-related health cannot be understood without complementing the framework based on waged employment with other frameworks related to gender roles and women's work in the domestic sphere. Both women and men are facing different risks due to the gender division of labour or they are exposed to the same risks in different degree.

Poor people frequently lack access to affordable, reliable, safe and environmentally benign sources of energy. This hinders their efforts to move out of poverty and seriously constrains their ability to improve their living situations. People without modern energy services must spend more of their time and physical energy on survival and, therefore, have fewer opportunities to pursue educational and income-generating activities.

Household energy and indoor air pollution pose a substantial vulnerability to the health of rural women and children. Use of biofuels for cooking in rural households in developing countries causes respiratory and other illnesses. It also has implications for household safety, allocation and use of the time of household members especially women, children below five years and local natural resource environment. Furthermore, indoor air pollution is a proxy indicator of inefficient use of limited sources of energy and household income. Biofuels are still the main source of energy for most of households in developing countries. There is strong evidence that chronic exposure to indoor air pollutants enhances the risk of a range of respiratory illnesses, including acute lower respiratory infections in children and chronic obstructive pulmonary disease in adults, essentially women.

This book basically focuses on economic and energy security from the perspective of rights to natural resources environment and their impact on livelihood security 'missing link' between poverty, job insecurity, environmental degradation and conflict. The long-term purpose is to mitigate conflict and promote work right and environmental security by improving livelihood security through strengthening the rights of natural resource dependent communities to the resources on which their livelihoods are based. The specific objective has been demonstrated the links between resource rights, livelihood and environmental security and depict policy recommendations.

Siddhartha Sarkar

Chapter - 1

Are Women more Vulnerable?

INTRODUCTION

The recent phenomenal intensification of the informal economy and the rising interaction and interdependence of the formal and informal economy lead to growing interest in studies of the informal economy among many researchers and policy makers. The term informal sector and informal economy are used interchangeably to specify that segment of the economy and labour market, which has absorbed significant numbers of job seekers and unemployed workers outside government regulations and formal systems of labour and social protection. Studying the existing literature on the informal economy rapidly makes it evident that there is no standardized conceptual framework wrapping the subject (Sarkar 2005). An extensive range of terms is used for numerous definitions or less precise descriptions of the phenomenon. Sometimes the similar term is used for diverse concepts and sometimes several terms portray the same concept. Various methods of research have been used to attain information on different concepts of the informal economy. The choice of methodology often resolves which part of the informal economy may be covered. This delves into why institutions or researchers interested in a specific definition and a specific coverage of the informal economy tend to use related approach and methodology. The scholars of the informal sector are still grappling with developing a concrete theoretical framework for what is undoubtedly a multifarious subject. However a key achievement of existing work on the sector is the legitimizing of the informal sector as a theoretical concept that calls for further empirical consideration. The theoretical framework has been useful to evaluate the manner in which the informal sector is conceptualized (Sarkar 2006a).

The concept of informal sector is not easy to define specifically. Most often it is defined negatively by indicating the nonexistence of characteristics that belong to formal activities, of special emphasis being labour market characteristics, security or regularity of work, better earnings, existence of non wage and long term benefits, protective legislation and union protection (Banerjee 1985; Papola 1980). Since a number of activities within the formal sector are getting informalised and private, small scale manufacturing units employing predominantly women labour is growing– the borderline becomes blurred. While earnings may still be better in the emerging formal sector, its major advantages in terms of non-wage and long term benefits, security and protection of work likely to be getting diluted (Eapen 2001). At the same time, within the informal sector itself, evidence discloses that a number of self-employment activities in the form of micro enterprises are undertaken with great ingenuity and entrepreneurial spirit and therefore have a growth potential (Rakowski 1994).

The term informal sector was first initiated by Keith Hart (1970) in a study of urban Ghana. He describes the informal sector as that part of the urban labour force, which falls outside the organized labour market. The study identified a number of incomes and employment generating activities in the un-enumerated sector of urban settlements. The workers involved in the un-enumerated sector mainly served as self-employed, as against the wageworkers in the enumerated sector. The new entrants to the urban labour market particularly migrants from rural areas were forced to work in the informal sector partly on account of lack of adequate opportunities in the formal sector and partly due to the workers' lack of skills and adequate experience required for the jobs in the formal sector. Keith Hart has used the terms, namely, informal income generating activities, unorganized sector, un-enumerated sector, self-employed individuals and urban proletariat in his study more or less alternatively and interchangeably. Thus, the informal sector is its identification with pre-capitalist mode of production, own account of workers and no access to the benefits of social security and is characterized by low capital intensity, low level of productivity, a tiny and usually poor clientele, a low level of formal schooling, intermediate technology, preponderance of family labour and ownership, ease of entrance and last but not least, lack of support and recognition from the government (Sarkar and Bhuimali 2005).

Emerging of more than two decades of surveys, the main features of informal sector economic units are ease of entry; small scale of the activity; self-employment, with a high proportion of family workers and apprentices; little capital and equipment; labour intensive technologies; low skills; low level of organization with no access to organized markets, to formal credit, to education and training or services and amenities; cheap provision of goods and services or provision of goods and services otherwise unavailable; low productivity and low incomes according to some analysts, or, on the contrary, incomes that are notably higher than in the public sector, especially during the recent period and in the context of structural adjustment policies, for other observers. Although these activities are legal, they rarely comply with official and administrative requirements. More specifically, as they often go unregistered, they do not pay relevant taxes, not only or not mostly out of a desire or willingness to escape and to remain concealed, but more likely because of the inability of governments to enforce often inadequate regulations. Informal sector activities are often tolerated as a kind of recognition that the laws are inadequate. Furthermore, they have become a means for many countries to cope with population growth, rural-urban migrations, economic crises, poverty and indebtedness. In addition, many formal wage earners are engaged in informal businesses held as additional jobs in order to compensate declining wages and purchasing powers. Thus, one cannot consider that there is a perfect dichotomy between participants in the informal sector on the one hand, and people who receive wages and salaries from Government, public and private modern sectors usually called the protected sector, on the other. The complexity and looseness of the concept explain why it has not been possible until now to reach an international agreement on a definition covering the variety of analytical purposes adopted by data users. For this reason labour statisticians have decided to distinguish the several definitions that may vary according to the need of users at the tabulation stage, from the one single statistical definition for the purpose of data collection.

For statistical purposes, the informal sector is regarded as a group of production units which form a part, within the System of National Accounts (1993), of the household sector as unincorporated enterprises owned by households. Household enterprises (or unincorporated enterprises owned by households) are distinguished from corporations and quasi-corporations on the basis of their legal status and the type of accounts they hold accordingly, household enterprises are not constituted as separate legal entities independently of the household or of household members that own them, and no complete set of accounts are available which could permit a clear distinction between the production activities of the enterprises and the other activities of their owners.

The informal sector is defined, irrespective of the kind of workplace, the extent of fixed capital assets, the duration of the activity of the enterprise and its operation as a main or secondary activity, as comprising of:

- Informal self-owned enterprises which may employ family workers, and employees on an occasional basis for operational purposes and depending on national circumstances, this segment comprises either all self-owned enterprises, or only those which are not registered under specific forms of national legislation (factories or commercial acts, tax or social security laws, professional groups, regulatory or similar acts, laws or regulations established by national legislative bodies).
- Enterprises of informal employers which may employ one or more employees on a continuous basis and which comply with one or both of the criteria as size of the establishment below a specified level of employment (defined on the basis of minimum size requirements embodied in relevant national legislation or other empirical or statistical practices, the choice of the upper size limit taking account of the coverage of statistical enquiries in order to avoid an overlap), non-registration of the enterprise or its employees.

Furthermore, and for practical purposes, the informal sector may and should be restricted to non-agricultural activities. Professionals and domestic workers are included in the informal sector as far as they comply with the definitional characteristics or criteria. Home-based workers are included if they are own-account or sub-contracting with other informal sector units. Non-market production is excluded. The value of this definition resides in the fact that it leans on existing practices for estimating informal employment at a national or macro-economic level. As to poverty and its measurement through the poverty line, many income-expenditures or budget-consumption surveys have been carried out over the past three decades, which have provided the necessary data for the measurement of a poverty line and of the share of population living below this poverty line in the informal economy. Using usual income-expenditures surveys to which belong the numerous priorities or integrated Social Dimension of Adjustment surveys, as well as the Living Standard Measurement Study surveys carried out under World Bank programmes, the poverty line is defined through a notion of relative poverty. However, relating indicators on the share of informal sector in the labour force or GDP remains a somewhat risky attempt, at least as risky in comparison with GNP per capita. A more interesting orientation seems to lie in the assessment of the structure of sources of income. If most of the estimates of poverty rely on the measurement of expenditures taken as more reliable than income, recent progress have been made in the measurement of income and it is more frequent to observe incomes higher than expenditures in some surveys– these development are due to recent efforts to measure incomes from informal sector, but also incomes from transfers, a major issue for the assessment of poverty.

EXAMINING INFORMAL WORK IN THE DEVELOPING COUNTRIES

In order to measure and assess the informal sector, the conceptual definition must be made operational. The way it is operationalized will depend on the measurement objectives. Thus, for example, if the aim is to measure or analyze informal employment, then labour force surveys can be used and the definition can be operationalized based on status in employment. If the aim is to measure the production of the informal economy, it may be more appropriate to use household income and expenditure surveys and to adopt an operational framework based on productive units. Most of the existing methods for assessing the size of the informal sector focus on the informal economics activities, but not all are suitable for differentiating between different types of activities within the informal economy. Three different approaches for measuring the size of the informal economy may be distinguished such as indirect estimation methods, direct estimation methods and the perceptions of informed economic agents. Indirect estimation methods are the most widely used approach for estimating the extent of the informal economy. Estimates of the extent of the informal economy derived by currency demand approach assume that the entire informal economy is a consequence of tax evasion, again not distinguishing between different activities within the informal economy.

In examining trends in labour force, unemployment and informal employment, it has been found that GNP per capita has decreased in most countries except in Asia, and when it did not, the increase was much lower than the dramatic growth of the labour force. Therefore, the urban unemployment rates have passed beyond two digits in North Africa and in sub-Saharan Africa and they are rapidly reaching this threshold in Latin America (Table 1).

Table 2 shows the share of women in total informal sector employment as well as their share in total labor force for selected countries. In most cases women's share is under half, which is explained by the fact that women constitute less than 50 percent of the labour force in all countries. It shows also that the share of women in informal sector is higher than their share in total labour force in most countries, implying that women are over-represented in this sector.

The available evidence from countries without exception point to the existence of gender disparity in incomes, not only as a whole but also among workers in different branches and employment status suggest that incomes vis-à-vis the quality of employment varies considerably even within the informal sector. Table 3 recapitulates some salient features from the above evidence. Comparison across countries is hazardous because the cut off line for remuneration has been chosen arbitrarily. One can of course attempt to define a common

Table 1
Trends in Labour Force, Unemployment and Informal Employment

Country	*Annual growth rate*		*Urban or national* unemploy-ment rate*	*Employment rate in the informal sector (3)*	
	GNP / cap 1980-93	*Labour force 1980-95*	*Years 1990*	*Years 1980*	*Years 1990*
North Africa	**10.0**	**3.0**	**15.8(1)**	**38.8(1)**	**43.4(1)**
Algeria	-0.8	3.8	20,5*	21.4	25.4
Morocco	1.2	2.6	12,0*	56.9	–
Tunisia	1.2	2.8	16,8*	36.0	39.3
Egypt	2.8	2.5	14,0*	58.7	65.3
Sub-Saharan Africa	**-1.4**	**2.5**	**16.0(1)(4)**	**68.1(1)**	**74.8(1)(4)**
Benin	-0.4	2.7	10.1	86.0	92.8
Burkina Faso	0.8	2.0	-	70.0	77.0
Chad	3.2	2.3	-	-	74.2
Guinea	-	2.2	12.3	64.4	71.9
Kenya	0.3	3.3	16.2	61.4	71.6
Mali	-1.0	2.4	9.9	63.1	78.6
Mauritania	-0.8	2.2	31.6	69.4	75.3
Mozambique	-1.5	1.6	-	-	73.5
Niger	-4.1	3.0	-	62.9	-
Senegal	-0.1	2.7	-	76.0	-
South Africa	-0.2	2.6	-	-	18.9
Zaire	-	2.9	-	59.6	-
Zambia	-	3.0	29.3	-	58.3
Latin America (2)	**-0.4**	**2.5**	**8.1(1)**	**52.3(1)**	**56.9(1)**
Argentina	-0.5	1.6	18.8	47.5	53.3
Bolivia	-0.7	2.6	3.6	56.9	63.6
Brazil	0.3	2.6	4.6	52.0	57.6
Colombia	1.5	3.5	9.0	55.2	55.5
Ecuador	1.5	3.4	6.9	51.2	53.5
Mexico	-0.5	3.2	6.3	55.5	59.4
Paraguay	-0.7	2.9	5.6	61.4	65.5
Venezuela	-0.7	3.3	10.3	38.8	46.9
Asia	-	**1.9**	**5.3**	**53.0**	**63.0**
India	3.0	1.9	-	76.2	73.7
Indonesia	6.8	2.8	7.2	39.2	77.9
Pakistan	3.1	3.1	6.1	39.0	64.6
Philippines	-0.6	2.7	7.4	-	66.9
Thailand	6.3	2.2	0.4	57.4	51.4
Iran	-0.2	3.3	-	-	43.5
Turkey	2.4	2.6	-	-	-

Source: Charmes [2001]

Notes: (1) Non-weighted arithmetical means (2) Informal employment estimates for 1990 and 1995 (3) As a share of total non-agricultural employment (4) Without South Africa

Table 2
Share of Women Employment in Informal Sector

Country	*Women's share in the informal sector*				*Women's share in total labour force per cent*
	Per cent	*Year*	*Per cent*	*Year*	
Latin America and the Caribbean					
Brazil	-	-	41	1990	28
Colombia	41	1984	43	1992	-
Costa Rica	24	1982	15	1984	22
Ecuador urban	37	1974	-	-	-
Mexico	36	1976	32	1992	28
Peru	46	1970	50	1985	-
Uruguay	-	-	34	1985	32
Venezuela	-	-	34	1992	28
Asia					
India	-	-	5	1977	-
Indonesia	-	-	48	1985	31
Malaysia	-	-	42	1986	36
Philippines	-	-	52	1988	-
Thailand	48	1988	48	1990	44
Africa					
Botswana	-	-	70	1984-85	-
Egypt	-	-	3	1986	10
Gambia	-	-	44	1983	39
Ghana	-	-	61	1970	-
Kenya	-	-	34	1982	-
Tanzania	40	1991	36	1995	16
Zambia	-	-	59	1986	30
Zimbabwe	-	-	58	1986	-

Source: United Nations [1995].

cut off line as is done in studies on poverty but it is perhaps less meaningful in this case as the labour market situation differs considerably not only across countries but also over time. In a large majority of cases more than half the female employment is of poor quality, irrespective of the fact whether they are self employed or wage workers.

Leaving aside the modern sector wage workers in Botswana and Abidjan who are small in numbers, and the case of Dar es Salaam mentioned already, in most of the cases the relative share of female employment in poor quality as indicated by a low level of income is at least twice as large as for men. For instance in La Paz the proportion of women in the informal sector with remuneration below one legal minimum wage (73.6 percent) is more than twice that of men (35.7 percent). Exceptions are piece rate workers in Bombay, sales workers in Malaysia, self employed in Lusaka, informal sector in Botswana and heads of informal enterprises in Abidjan; in these cases a large proportion of men are also in poor quality employment (Table 3).

GENDER IMPACT ANALYSIS

In economy two types of work exist namely, paid work and unpaid work. While a worker is engaged for performing chore on the basis of an agreed wage payment, the activities carried out by the concerned worker may be termed as paid work. On the other hand, the time spent by a worker in several activities in domestic sector may be termed as unpaid care work. In economy unpaid work is often informal while paid work may be formal or informal. The connections between the unpaid care economy and the paid economy (Himmelweit 2002) are represented in Figure 1, which shows the flows of the characteristic net contribution of each sector to the rest of the economy. The unpaid economy consists of the domestic sector that contributes to individual socialization and to the production and maintenance of human capabilities. The paid economy contains both the social and economic infrastructure and producing sector. However, each sector may and does make other outputs.

Gender impact analysis must examine the effects of any economic policy on both the paid and unpaid economies, disaggregating these effects by gender. The most significant gender division of labour is that between the two economies.

Table 3
Employment Quality: Gender Disparity in Informal Sector

Country / city / area / year	*Income*	*Percent of employment*	
		Male	*Female*
Mexico urban 1993			
All workers in informal sector	one minimum wage	11.5	28.3
Bolivia (La Paz) 1983			
All workers in informal sector	one minimum wage	35.7	73.6
Brazil urban 1970			
Self employed	150 Crz. per month	25.4	69.5
Wage workers	150 Crz. per month	20.2	52.9
India (Bombay slums) 1979			
Self employed Wage workers	Rs. 150 per month	19.1	43.7
India (Bombay) 1990	Rs. 150 per month	25.9	69.3
Self employed	Rs.300 per week	39.1	79.5
Regular wage workers	Rs.300 per week	28.2	76.7
Piece rate workers	Rs.300 per week	70.6	97.8
India (six cities) 1988			
All workers in informal sector	One rupee per hour	13.5	50.8
Malaysia urban 1970			
Self employed	130 M$ per month	33.3	75.1
Wage workers	130 M$ per month	33.3	65.1
Sales workers	130 M$ per month	50.1	82.0
Service workers	130 M$ per month	37.5	79.1
Production workers	130 M$ per month	38.4	90.9
Zambia (Lusaka) 1974			
Self employed	60 Kwacha per month	51.3	86.1
Botswana 1984-85			
All workers in informal sector	50 Pula per month	44.1	67.1
Ivory Coast (Abidjan) 1984			
Heads of informal enterprises	25000 F.CFA per month	56.9	80.1
Wage workers modern sector			
Tanzania (Dar es Salaam) 1995	25000 F.CFA per month	5.4	1.0
Entrepreneurs-informal	30000 T Sh. per month	39.3	43.3

Source: Sethuraman [1998].

Women still devote the majority of their working time to the unpaid economy and men devote theirs to the paid economy in both developed and developing countries (United Nations Development Programme 1995). Given this disparity, the overall distributional effect of policies that improve the conditions of paid work over unpaid work will be to worsen gender inequality, unless those policies are specifically targeted on improving women's situation. Thus there are two aspects to the gender division of labour between paid and unpaid economies. It is not only that woman overall tend to do more unpaid caring work than men. It is also that an inside division of labour within households allocates that work and if a woman shares her household with another member, it is likely that that other member does less unpaid caring work than she does. This is not of course exact for women who share their household with other women, although the allocation of caring work may in practice still be unequal. A woman or anyone doing the bulk of caring work can lose bargaining power because her contribution of unpaid labour is less visible than her counterpart's economic contribution.

A United Nations (1991) report on women's work patterns based on surveys made across countries of the world gives a summary of women's devotion of time to both paid and unpaid economic activity. The findings are as under:

- Women spend more of their time working than men folk in all developed and developing regions except northern America and Australia where the working hours are almost equal.
- In developing countries women spent more time in the labour force than their household work. Men by contrast are spending less amount of time working in the labour force than before in all developed regions and slightly increasing amounts of time in housework in northern America, Australia and Western Europe.
- In Africa, Asia and the Pacific women work as an average 12-13 hours more than men per week.
- Men in developing regions generally do less household chores than men in the developed regions.
- Women everywhere in the world have nearly total responsibility for household work. While men 'help out' women retain the responsibility of housework.

This analysis suggests some criteria by which policy makers should evaluate the gender impact of economic policy. These criteria do not incorporate policy goals in themselves, but suggest considerations to which policy makers should give attention in order that economic goals can be pursued efficiently while making visible unintended inequitable consequences. These criteria are designed to make explicit when economic policy conforms or conflicts with other policy objectives, including the promotion of equal opportunities throughout society for men and women. Although economic policy should in general be designed to reinforce rather than undermine other policy objectives, it is also important to recognize where conflicts between objectives occur in order to try to resolve them.

Figure 1
The Interdependence of the Paid and Unpaid Economies

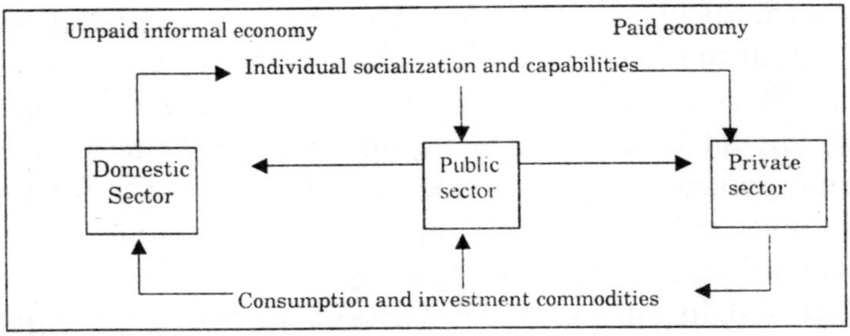

Source: Himmelweit [2002].

The policy makers should assess the effects of their policies on both paid and unpaid caring economies. In particular, it should be made explicit when policies are not broadly neutral with respect to paid and unpaid work, and the cost of any incentives being provided to either paid or unpaid work should be justified. When the effect is to encourage movement into the paid economy, the social consequences of any reduction in the output of care from the unpaid economy and/or any increase in total working time for those continuing to work in the unpaid economy must be assessed. When additional unpaid work results, the gender distribution of such work and its effect on individuals' opportunities to take paid work and contribute elsewhere in the economy must be assessed; the cost of adequate compensation for such extra work should be considered in assessing the net benefits to society. Although time and money are not interchangeable, an evaluation of the effects of any policy on people's time should be integrated with any assessment of financial effects. Where wage rates cannot be used, estimates for the value of unpaid work can be derived from those used in constructing household satellite accounts, where available. This evaluation should be at the overall societal level and broken down by gender. Distributional effects between households and between individuals within households should also be assessed. The distribution between men and women of the effects on both economies must be assessed. Such assessment involves three elements namely, the extent to which policies reinforce or break down gender inequalities in the division of time between paid and unpaid work should be taken into account; ideally polices should encourage economic autonomy and choice equally for men and women in both paid and unpaid work, the extent to which policies promote or undercut equality within paid work should be assessed. In particular, the effects of any changes in unpaid work responsibilities on the conditions under which men and women enter the labor market should be considered, and the extent to which policies promote sharing of unpaid work between men and women should be assessed. In particular, the extent to which policies enable employment to be combined with caring responsibilities is relevant to this criterion. Gender equality should be assessed both between households and within them. It is important to know the gender composition of households that are gaining and households that are losing overall from proposed policy changes; in addition, analysis should focus on whether the changes reinforce or break down the disadvantages experienced by certain types of households. It is important to know how women and men are faring within their households; in particular it is important to know whether changes would reinforce or help to break down existing gender inequalities in money, work, and power within households. Both of these issues should be assessed in terms of time as well as money.

CONCLUDING REMARKS

The informal workers may be secluded and transitory; there is a lot of fear due to the insecurity of work and lack of legal protection as to the effectiveness of being part of a union. The flexibility offered by more informal work arrangements has been viewed as potentially assenting for women workers due to the limitation of alternative job opportunities for them in the formal sector. In general the informalisation of work has had a negative impact on women workers and has meant low wages, job insecurity, isolation and lack of opportunities to organize. The informal economy is a part of survival and household strategies especially for the poor; nevertheless its contribution to well being remains inadequately understood and largely unnoticed by policy makers.

Nevertheless, the lack of formal employment coupled with an inability to meet household needs in the absence of welfare benefits or because of the inadequacy of the available assistance, encourages people to turn to the informal economy in response. Likewise perceive the informal employment strategies of the unemployed as a part of a survival strategy, through which some individuals develop alternative ways of working in the face of the existing limited opportunities and the failure of the welfare system. Informality enables the unemployed poor to get some basic income, but what is more important; it may help them maintain a sense of self-confidence. Most individuals work in the informal sector only if they have to or if they can supplement their informal sector earnings with their unemployment benefits and the social services, such as health care, that are available with these benefits. First of all, for the vast majority, informal sector wages are very low. The more illegal the work, the higher the wages, as well as the higher risks and fines if caught. In turn high taxes depress economic activity and income stabilization, which brings us back to square one, making informality a mechanism of survival and coping, especially for the poor. Many poor people observe the lack of fair access to the legal system and the lack of security as major components of poverty. The lack of trust in the legal system and the possibility for people to have influence on it in a non-transparent way are major issues (Sarkar 2006b).

REFERENCES

Banerjee, N. (1985), *Women Workers in the Unorganized Sector,* Sangam Books, Hyderabad.

Charmes, J. (2001), *Informal Sector, Poverty and Gender: A Review of Empirical Evidence,* Background Paper for the World Development Report 2001, Washington DC.

Eapen, M. (2001), Women in Informal Sector in Kerala: Need for Re-examination, *Economic and Political Weekly*, XXXVI (20): 2390-2392.

Hart, K. (1970), Small Scale Entrepreneurs in Ghana and Development Planning, *The Journal of Development Studies*, 6 (4): 104-120.

Himmelweit, S. (2002), Making Visible the Hidden Economy: The Case for Gender Impact Analysis of Economic Policy, *Feminist Economics*, 8(1): 49-70.

Papola, T.S. (1980), Informal Sector: Concept and Policy, *Economic and Political Weekly*, 15 (8): 817-823.

Rakowski, C.A. (1994), Convergence and Divergence in the Informal Sector Debate: A Focus on Latin America, 1984-92, *World Development*, 22 (4): 501-516.

Sethuraman, S.V. (1998), *Gender, Informality and Poverty: A Global Review,* World Bank, Washington D.C.

System of National Accounts (1993), *System of National Accounts 1993,* World Bank, Washington, D.C.

United Nations (1995), *The World's Women 1995: Trends and Statistics,* New York.

Sarkar, S. (2005), The Conceptual and Theoretical Framework of Informal Economy: A Review of Literature in Developed and Developing Countries, *Journal of Social and Economic Policy*, 2(2): 187-205.

Sarkar, S. and Bhuimali, A. (2005), *Disadvantaged Women in Informal Sector,* Abhijeet Publications, Delhi.

Sarkar, S. (2006a), *Theorising Informal Economy,* Abhijeet Publications, Delhi.

Sarkar, S. (2006b), *Women Struggle for Sustainability,* Serials Publications, New Delhi..

United Nations (1991), *The World's Women 1970-1990,* New York.

United Nations Development Programme (1995), *Human Development Report 1995,* Oxford University Press, Oxford.

Chapter - 2

Energy, Livelihood and Poverty

INTRODUCTION

Poverty is one of the most fundamental issues, and urgently needs to be addressed. Moving people out of poverty forms a basis of much international development policy (Sarkar 2005a). In almost all of the South Asian countries there exists absolute poverty. There are high rates of poverty among rural people, indigenous South Asian and some groups of immigrants. It negatively affects the life chances and opportunities of women and children. Children are vulnerable and dependent, and the effects and impacts of poverty can so easily stultify and distort women and children future lives by robbing them of opportunities to develop their potential. Poverty can be measured in different ways. It is often expressed in relation to a poverty line, a defined income level that is updated regularly. Each measure has advantages and disadvantages, and slightly different methods of estimate and updating may fabricate somewhat different results. As well as measuring family incomes, it is useful to consider the distribution of assets or wealth, which might offer some protection in the event of an income crunch such as hasty unemployment or prolonged illness. People living on low incomes report poor health and the incidence of illness at much higher rates than people on high incomes. This can be due to stress, crowded housing and poor nutrition. Poverty can also lead to homelessness. Both the shortage of low-cost private rental accommodation and continuing high levels of unemployment affect people's ability to pay the rent. Members of families with low incomes often have limited educational opportunities, leading to much narrower employment options. It can also contribute to poor self-esteem and less participation in society. In this way poverty and social exclusion can affect successive generations.

According to the World Energy Assessment, energy services are indispensable for human survival and development. They play a critical role across the whole spectrum of development activities. Of the three billion people living in rural areas in developing countries today, nearly 2 billion still have neither access to nor can pay for modern energy carriers, such as electricity and/or liquid or gaseous fuels. These energy carriers are to provide essential energy services such as heating for cooking, motive power, lighting and cooling (refrigeration), thus seriously reducing the income opportunities and quality of life. Access to electricity and other modern energy sources is a necessary, but not a sufficient, requirement for economic and social development. The escape from poverty also requires, among other things, clean water, adequate sanitation and health services, a good education system and a communication network. Yet cheap and available energy is indispensable. Electricity provides the best and most efficient form of lighting; household appliances require it. Kerosene and liquefied petroleum gas (LPG) are more energy-efficient cooking fuels than traditional biomass.

The concentration of indoor air pollutants coming out from combustion of biofuels such as wood, agriculture crops and dung cake used by rural households in developing countries cause severe health problems especially to women and children below five years. Mothers and their children spend an average of six hours per day in highly polluted indoor areas It has been estimated that approximately half the global population and up to 90 per cent of rural households in developing countries still rely on biomass fuels and about 75 per cent of Indian households use biofuels for cooking purposes (Sarkar 2005b). Typically cooked indoors in open fires or poorly functioning stoves, which leads to levels of air pollution that are among the highest ever measured. Therefore indoor air pollution with biofuels is an issue that requires to be addressed through gender, energy, environment and health policy. Some of highest concentrations of pollutants come about due to the use of biofuels for cooking in rural indoor environment (Sarkar 2004). In developed countries transformation has without exception been come with by a shift from biofuels to petroleum products (kerosene, LPG) and electricity. In developing countries even where cleaner more sophisticated fuels are available, households often continue to use biomass (Smith 1987). Although the portion of global energy derived from biofuel has fallen substantially which is evidence that biofuels use is increasing among the poor. Poverty is one of the main hurdles to the adoption of cleaner fuels and slow pace of development in many countries implies that biofuels will continue to be used by the poor for many years. Poor people frequently lack access to affordable, reliable, safe and environmentally benign sources of energy. This hinders their efforts to move out of poverty and seriously constrains their ability to improve their living situations. People without modern energy services must spend more of their time and physical energy on survival and, therefore, have fewer opportunities to pursue educational and income-generating activities. Limited access to energy is also a problem that has a disproportionate effect on women, especially in rural areas. Rural women spend up to 25 per cent of their time carrying heavy loads of fuel over increasingly long distances, at great risk to their health and safety. Therefore the vulnerable women suffer from the larger level of bribes than the non-poor households. With the difficult economic conditions of transition, a number of women no longer value edification as much as they did before the transition; their pinnacle priority is mere survival. In most ethnicity, women and men have differing roles and responsibilities according to socially defined division of labour based on gender. This gender inequity is reflected in a variety of social and economic dimensions. In terms of reproductive activities, women generally have primary responsibility for the care and feeding of children and families, as well as health care and education. In many developing countries, it is the women who perform most of the work related to subsistence agriculture, plus gathering and managing fuel and water as a part of the household responsibility. Their productive activities are often unpaid and labour-intensive. When women in rural areas do generate income, it tends to be within the informal sector, and not adequately reflected in national accounting systems. This serves to under-represent the importance of energy as an input to women's economic activities. Because they operate mostly in the informal and unpaid sectors, poor women have less access to financial resources, credit and equipment than do men, and less of a voice in household, or community-level, decision making. Gender-poverty is a problem that has a disproportionate effect on women and girls, especially in rural areas. The most obvious factors relate to time and physical effort. Many women in developing countries have to spend long hours gathering fuel and hauling water, using their own labour to carry heavy loads over long distances in addition to other informal work. When women are overburdened, they are more likely to keep their daughters home from school to assist with own household activities, including fuel and water collection, thereby limiting opportunities for girls to move forward through education, and rising the likelihood that their families will remain in poverty.

ENERGY AND VULNERABILITY

In South Asia, millions of women spend hours a day carrying fuel and water, taking away valuable time for other activities. Women in rural areas in South Asia are at the bottom rung of the so-called energy ladder, which associates users of progressively cleaner, more efficient fuels with corresponding higher levels of income. It is a situation that is both a determinant and a manifestation of poverty and inequitable gender relations. Traditional biomass (dung, agriculture residues and fuel wood) is at the bottom rung of the ladder for cooking, with charcoal, then kerosene and finally liquid petroleum gas (LPG) and electricity are towards the top. Traditional rural energy systems are characterized by the use of biomass, in the form of wood, plant residues, dung for heating and cooking, and human energy and or animal energy for motive power. Majority of household energy requirements are biomass energy for cooking. Human energy, measured in energy units, constitutes a small proportion of energy resources consumed compared to other sources. But the labour of women and children are indispensable in making the energy chain work such as the extraction/ collection of biomass to its transformation into an energy service such as heat for cooking. The extraction, transport, processing, conversion and distribution are the responsibility and the work of women, girls and boys primarily, according to the social norms which prescribe which activities are the obligations of women and which are those of men. Women are also at the bottom rung of another energy ladder for motive force. They depend entirely on their own motive force and are normally without any other resources such as animal power, mechanical or electrical devices for such energy transformations. Even where animal power and/or mechanical equipment are available in the household, gender norms, relations of power and division of labour tend to exclude women from use and certainly ownership and control of these assets. This energy situation has tremendous survival and developmental implications since the tasks associated with food preparation are critical to the prevailing agricultural systems. Small landowners engaged in agricultural production make up about three quarters of the rural population. Their production, the main source of rural livelihood and income, is primarily based on human and animal energy that is on muscle power. This motive power requires the biological conversion and storage of food into useful energy. Food intake, crucial for the daily reproduction of human energy for agricultural labour, in turn depends on processing and preparing the food harvested or gathered. The frequent, repetitive tasks associated with post-harvest food preparation, such as provisioning for water, firewood, grinding grain, pressing cooking oil and processing other ingredients are women's responsibilities and obligations. These are in addition to women's other labour inputs in agricultural production and in gathering the wild resources used in food preparation, oil and soap making and other household provisioning needs. Dependence on such traditional energy systems leads to multiple social and economic costs, which are overwhelmingly borne by poor women. Linked to the lower energy efficiency of fuel wood combustion is the higher emission of sulphur, carbon dioxide and particulates, pollutants resulting from incomplete combustion. The occupational hazards for women and for their young children from exposure to indoor air pollution, smoke and particulates when cooking are the negative impacts in terms of health burns, acute respiratory infections, lung disease, internal disorders and eye problems. Load carrying of fuel and other materials, for example in palm oil processing takes a health toll in terms of injury, miscarriages, and fatigue. Poor women in particular pay a disproportionate price for energy services not only because of the inefficiency and associated health costs. Long hours are spent collecting water and firewood for food preparation and agro processing, as well as the multiple other tasks that sustain rural livelihoods. The arduous and time-consuming nature of women's activities in such energy systems has significant opportunity costs in terms of other activities. These are agricultural production and other productive and income generating uses of time and energy, as well as time and energy for child care, health, education, rest, social and cultural activities, recreation and personal maintenance. As traditional fuel wood sources and water get increasingly scarce, the costs in terms of women's time and energy become more severe. This can also mean that they need to generate cash to buy firewood that is no longer possible to collect individually and this cash generation in its turn takes time and energy, including marketing time. Widening access to modern energy services can be a catalyst for sustainable human development, given these patterns of energy uses. But increased income is necessary to be able to afford to climb another rung of the energy ladder and release human time and energy for human development purposes. However this increased income is not possible without spending further time and human energy, when usage levels are already very high. Such is the energy-poverty trap which women in South Asia, in particular are struggling to get out of.

The relationship between gender and poverty is a complex and controversial issue that is now being discussed more than ever before. Although much policymaking has been informed by the idea of feminization of poverty, the precise nature of the nexus between gender and poverty needs to be better understood and operationalized in policymaking. The difficulty originates from the different shapes and forms gender inequalities and poverty take depending on the economic, social and ideological context. Yet another difficulty involves the scarcity of gender disaggregated data for a number of South Asian countries. For the last three decades, many women advocates have been arguing that women are poorer than men. The most common empirical expression of this idea is the concept of feminization of poverty. This idea has become popular both in shaping analyses of poverty and poverty alleviation strategies. Thus, targeting women has become one means for gender-sensitive poverty alleviation. Poor women have become the explicit focus of policymaking, for example, in the areas of micro credit programmes and income generation activities. However, the universal validity of the feminization of poverty is being empirically challenged. Although the idea that there are gender differences in experiences of poverty is not abandoned, a more nuance and complex analysis of poverty and gender inequalities is emerging. This, in turn, is giving rise to a more gender-aware approach to poverty elimination strategies.

In the literature on poverty, one frequently posed question is: are women poorer than men? In these discussions, the concept of feminization of poverty is used as a short hand for a variety of ideas. It can mean either one or a combination of the following.

- Women compared to men have a higher incidence of poverty.
- Women's poverty is more severe than men's.
- Over time, the incidence of poverty among women is increasing compared to men.

In addressing women's poverty, many studies measure the incidence of income or consumption poverty among female-headed households and compare it to that of male-headed counterparts. The unit of analysis is the household and the incidence of women's poverty is conflated with the poverty of men. On a priori grounds, there are reasons to be concerned about the welfare of female-headed households, since women are subject to discrimination in labour, credit and a variety of other markets and they own less property compared to men. In some societies, widows, divorced or abandoned women may be subject to social exclusion, isolation and harassment, making it very difficult for them to maintain a livelihood for themselves or their children. Women heads of households with young children may face great time constraints and may have to limit their work hours. Even though female-headed households are a relatively small proportion of households. This has been seen as evidence that women are becoming poorer over time relative to men. The comparative poverty of female-headed households vis-à-vis male-headed counterparts is not universal. It has also been argued that it may be more meaningful to study female-maintained households as opposed to those headed by women. Female-maintained households are those in which women are the primary providers of the family. What is also necessary to understand is the process through which households become women-headed or female-maintained rather than viewing headship as a static indicator. When programmes targeting female-headed households analyze the reasons for the rise, nature and vulnerability of such households, it has been possible to design effective anti-poverty programmes that target female headship.

ENGENDERING POVERTY

The household-headship approach in the studies of gender inequalities and poverty resulted from the fact that the household has been the unit of analysis for studying poverty and female headship was the only gender-transparent factor in this approach. This line of research has been very useful in revealing characteristics of households associated with the gender of household heads, such as differences in dependency ratios and time constraints. However, it also had the effect of disguising other types of linkages between gender and poverty. For example, it failed to address the poverty experienced by women in non-poor households resulting from gender bias in the distribution of resources within households. Thus, gendered analysis of poverty need to go beyond household-headship approach. At the microeconomic level, there is a need to understand the gender and age based power relations within households, the mechanisms of cooperation and conflict as well as the dynamics of bargaining that shape the distribution of work, income and assets. Such processes of bargaining do not take place in a social vacuum, however. They are affected by social norms as well as the differential access to opportunities and resources men and women have outside the household. Therefore, the analysis also needs to be extended to the meso level, where the interaction of households and household members with a variety of other economic and social institutions such as the state or markets is studied. Often institutions, which are not inherently gender biased, are nonetheless bearers of gender bias. In a similar vein, engendering the macroeconomic level of analysis is equally important since the economic, social, political and ecological environments in which households maintain themselves or fall into destitution are shaped by macroeconomic policies (Sen 1990).

Poverty has been traditionally understood to mean a lack of access to resources, productive assets and income resulting in a state of material deprivation. Emphasizing deficiency in private consumption, poverty has been defined as private consumption per person falling below a particular level. In this approach, absolute rather than relative poverty has been the focus of attention. Recently, the concept of poverty and the discussion of its causal explanations have been broadened. As the consumption/income approach to defining poverty has come under increased criticism, it has been suggested that in the analysis of poverty common property resources and state-provision of commodities should be taken into account and the concept of poverty should be broadened to include lack of dignity and autonomy. The inclusion of the latter in the meaning of poverty draws from the insight that being non-poor implies a freedom from the necessity to perform activities that are regarded as subservient and (their) ability to choose self-fulfilling and rewarding life styles. In these increasingly multidimensional conceptualizations, poverty is being viewed as a process, rather than as a static concept. For example, the poor, rather than being viewed as passive victims of society in need of handouts, are viewed as agents who struggle to cope with poverty with whatever assets they may posses. The emphasis is on the assets they own and resources they can access rather than on what they lack. Along these lines, in the literature that focuses on the coping mechanisms of the poor, the concept of assets has been extended to include social capital and household relations (Moser 1996). Furthermore, new qualitative, as opposed to quantitative, approaches to poverty assessment have emphasized the poor own criteria of poverty as well as their own solutions (Chambers 1996). The policy implications of this new approach have emphasized programmes that enable the poor to exercise their agency, their own solutions and creativity by creating an enabling environment as well as making available critical external resources such as credit. Empowerment of the poor is viewed as critical to the success of poverty elimination. Another recent approach, the social exclusion approach, emphasizes the importance of institutions and norms that exclude certain groups from a variety of social networks and the importance of social solidarity in sustaining livelihoods. These new insights on poverty have far reaching implications for analyzing the gendered nature of poverty as well as the relationship between gender inequalities and overall poverty levels. Add to, UNDP has contributed to these efforts both by broadening the discussions around the conceptualizations and measurements/assessments of poverty as well as by introducing new approaches to poverty elimination policies. Particularly, the capabilities/entitlements approach spearheaded by Sen, which constitutes the analytical basis of UNDP's Human Development Reports and the concept of Sustainable Human Development have helped broaden the understanding of poverty and vulnerability. According to this perspective, poverty represents the absence of some basic capabilities to function. Functioning, in turn, represent the doings and beings of a person. Thus, the capability approach reconciles the notions of absolute and relative poverty, since relative deprivation in incomes and commodities can lead to an absolute deprivation in minimum capabilities (UNDP 1997). UNDP bases the concept of human poverty, which was introduced in the 1997 Human Development Report, on the capabilities approach. As distinct from income poverty, human poverty refers to the denial of opportunities and choices for living a most basic or tolerable human life. It, therefore, takes into account more than the minimum necessities for material well-being and views poverty as multidimensional. The Human Poverty Index (HPI), also introduced in the same report, measures deprivation in basic human development i.e., a short life, lack of basic education and lack of access to public and private resources. Although human poverty is related to income poverty, the two concepts are not the same. Measurements of income poverty, such as the head-count ratio (HCR), focus on levels of absolute income poverty, while the HPI focuses on capabilities such as access to clean water, health services and the level of literacy. Focusing on the concept of human poverty helps us to see the causes of poverty, not merely its symptoms. Quantitative measures such as the HCR implicitly treat households as harmonious units and limit our understanding of gender and poverty. Just as growth based approaches to poverty alleviation assume that the benefits of growth automatically trickle down to poor households, consumption/income approaches to poverty assessment assume that the benefits of an income increase in poor households trickle down to all members equally. However, households exhibit conflict and inequality as well as cooperation and sharing. Thus, the concept of human poverty has been helpful in shedding light on the relationship between gender inequalities and poverty. Although households are still very important as units of poverty analysis, the human poverty concept makes it possible to disaggregate the household and analyze the relative poverty or well being of household members. Such an approach focuses the discussion on gender differences in deprivation in basic education (illiteracy) health services and life expectancy (short lives) and the socially constructed constraints on the choices of various groups such as women or lower castes. Poverty eradication is an aspect of human development, which is defined as a process of enlarging people's choices (UNDP 1990).

From a human poverty or capabilities perspective, makes it possible to see that women are indeed poorer in most societies in many dimensions of capabilities such education and health, but not necessarily in terms of life expectancy, although there are also societies in which women's life expectancy is shorter than men's due to maternal mortality or child mortality that may result from biases against girls' health and nutrition needs. Resource allocation within households is often biased against girls and women. In addition, it is harder for women to transform their capabilities into incomes or well being. Gender inequalities in the distribution of income, access to productive inputs such as credit, command over property or control over earned income, as well as gender biases in labour markets and social exclusion that women experience in a variety of economic and political institutions form the basis for the greater vulnerability of women to chronic poverty. Across a wide range of cultures and levels of economic development, women tend to specialize in unpaid reproductive or caring labour compared to men, who tend to specialize in paid production activities. Women's combined paid and unpaid labour time is greater than men's (UNDP 1997). Although it is often stated that labour is the poor most abundant asset, women are relatively time poor and much of their work is socially unrecognized since it is unpaid. Furthermore, when women are in paid work, the return to their labour is lower than the return to men's labour. Thus, women on average work more, but have less command over income as well as assets. Nor do they always have control or command over their own labour. In some cases, men may prohibit their wives from working outside the household and seclude them. In other cases, men may extract labour from women with the threat or actuality of violence, as for instance, in the case of unpaid women family labourers. Men tend to have more command over women's labour so that in crisis situations they may be able to mobilize the labour of women, while women generally do not have the reciprocal right or ability to mobilize men's labour. Women's responsibilities for reproductive labour limit the range of paid economic activities they can undertake. Women are less mobile than men because of their reproductive/caring labour activities and because of social norms that restrict their mobility in public. In the paid sphere, they tend to be concentrated in informal labour activities (such as home working), since such activities allow them to combine paid work with unpaid reproductive labour. However, these are also insecure forms of work. It is hard for such workers to get organized for collective action. The gender-based division of labour between unpaid (and often reproductive labour) and paid labour renders women economically and socially more insecure and vulnerable to not only chronic poverty but also to transient poverty that can result from familial, personal or social and economic crises, including those that arise from macroeconomic policies, political and ethnic conflict situations or health-related crises such as the HIV/AIDS epidemics. Yet, in such crises, as in the case of structural adjustment policies and macroeconomic crises, women work harder compared to men and increase their paid and unpaid labour activities to maintain their households (Moser 1996). This is not to argue that the stake is always loaded against women in general and poor women, in particular. For example, the feminization of labour in paid work associated with structural adjustment policies implies that women potentially can have greater control over income within the household. This can lead to an increased bargaining power for women within the household and is therefore potentially empowering. However, this comes at the expense of increased time poverty. The concept of multidimensionality of poverty makes it clear that poor people often face trade-offs between different dimensions of poverty in their struggle with deprivation. However, women face many more such trade-offs compared to men as their economic choices are more socially constrained and as their work burden is almost universally higher. Although it is clear that poor women should not be viewed as passive victims and their agency should be recognized, gender relations and inequalities cause women and men to experience poverty differently within households.

Thus, the new approaches to the conceptualization of poverty and the recent popularity of participatory approaches to poverty assessment have helped us recognize how women are poorer in a multiplicity of dimensions of poverty and how they experience poverty differently than men. This does not mean that quantitative methods are useless or necessarily gender biased. Both the qualitative and the quantitative methods are as gender biased as the user of the methods (Kabeer 1996). While the quantitative methods have their limitations from a gender perspective as pointed out above, qualitative methods such as Participatory Poverty Assessments (PPA), which is an approach that defines poverty through the eyes of the poor using the criteria that poor people themselves put forth, must also be carefully designed. Such assessments must be gender aware in the sense of including women's and men's views, without assuming that the needs of poor men and poor women coincide or that the assessments of poor women and poor men about poverty and their needs about poverty elimination are the same. There may also be reasons for participatory approaches to be gender biased since sometimes it may be more difficult for women to voice their views publicly or the local patriarchal ideology may be held similarly by men and women shaping views of both groups about study of four poor urban communities in the developing countries, Moser (1996) found that the principle coping response to economic crisis is the mobilization of women's and children's labour. In three of the communities women and men performed the same amount of paid labour, but women did much more unpaid labour compared to men. In all four cases women's combined labour burden was higher than men's. Women increased their paid work often in the informal sector. Girls tended to take over the domestic work responsibilities of mothers, while boys tended to be mobilized into paid labour. Thus, girls' labour was also less visible. The gender-based earnings differentials in the informal sector are greater than those in the formal sector and feminization of the labour force under crisis conditions can lead to further deterioration of women's position in labour markets. The economic empowerment of women and capacity building for transformatory change has been emphasized in South Asia Poverty Alleviation Programme (SAPAP) supported by United Nations Development Programme (UNDP).

SAPAP started in 1994 as UNDP's effort to support South Asian countries in eradicating poverty. Bangladesh, India and Nepal were chosen as pilot areas for a programme of social mobilization through participatory community organizations of the poor. In 1996, a larger programme was formulated to include pro-poor macro-policy initiatives and participatory poverty monitoring components in its framework, and it was expanded to include Sri Lanka, Pakistan and Maldives in its implementation area. The social mobilization component is the most critical element of the SAPAP and the synergy among the three components makes it a unique project. UNDP's contribution to social mobilization has been the promotion of experiential learning to demonstrate the effectiveness of appropriate models of social mobilization for scaling-up poverty alleviation efforts and improved participatory development planning.

In India, since 1994, the project has been under implementation in three districts of Andhra Pradesh, which are characterized by high level of social stratification with high levels of poverty, caste differentiation, severe ecological degradation, landlessness and landlordism, poor transport infrastructure, high prevalence of child labour, child marriage, high underemployment due to droughts, low wages, high infant mortality and recurring epidemics like measles. According to participatory poverty assessments, households with female heads, single parents and elderly with no support mechanisms are extremely poor. More than 50 per cent of the households covered by the project are below poverty line.

The approach taken on in India views the poor as agents and partners in the effort of poverty reduction, recognizing the creativity of the poor and their capacity for enterprise and accords them respect and dignity as partners in development. Based on these premises, the project has been building associations and groups to help unite the poor at both intra and inter village levels. The groups at the village level are called self help groups (SHGs), averaging around 16 members. The SHGs federate into Village Development Organizations (VDO). The VDOs in turn unite into mandal level organizations. As of August 1997 there were 2,458 SHGs with 40,720 members and almost all (98 per cent) were women's associations. Most groups are caste based.

The main focus of activity of the SHGs is to generate savings for income generating projects in the village. The seed capital is provided by the UNDP. With its focus on the landless poor and small farmers, the seed capital is intended to increase the resource base of the poor and gradually enable them to cross the poverty line. At the end of August 1997 the total amount of seed capital was Rs. 10 million, the total amount of savings accumulated through the SHGs was Rs. 21.43 million and another Rs. 5.1 million was provided by the government and NGOs. Thus, the total amount of loans given out was Rs. 36.5 million. More than a half of the total amount of loans (52 per cent) was given for health, education and consumption; areas which women are in need the most, the rest were used for directly productive purposes.

The project has pioneered a unique participatory method for the identification of projects as well as beneficiaries at the grassroots level in the true sprit of planning from below. Although the entry point of the project is mainly credits and savings, the SHGs benefit the people in every aspect of life in a village community. The groups are instrumental, first in collectively identifying problems and the people or groups mostly affected by them, second in coming up with different alternatives i.e., projects as possible solutions, and finally in selecting the most suitable projects from those possible alternatives. The groups have shown enormous sensitivity to those extremely poor in the selection of female-headed households, deserted women, landless labourers, and families facing health or other problems. Thus, SHGs differ from the more traditional micro credit programmes in that it is the group members who identify the problems, the possible solutions and projects and the allocation of loans according to criteria set by themselves.

The activities of the SHGs generated considerable advances in women's empowerment both quantitatively and qualitatively. The provision and redistribution of funds created a great support for the most vulnerable groups, the majority of which are poor women. However, the SHGs, and hence the overall project, is more beneficial in its qualitative and long-term capacity building effect on women's empowerment. The project helped women demonstrate their very high level of awareness. The collective activities under the roof of SHGs set in motion the extraordinary leadership and management skills of women. The women members report that the opportunity to save provided them with a sense of security and access to consumption and emergency loans, which has released them from subservience to money lenders, who charge extremely high interest rates. This, they point out, has given them back their self dignity. They have gained new recognition and a new status in the community as they attended the SHG meetings and voiced their opinions on economic issues. The collaborative and positive relationships among the women members have contributed to the emergence of mutual trust and a sense of security among them. They have also gained respect in the eyes of their husbands and in laws as they brought tangible benefits to the entire family. Men have started to appreciate the collective power of women in tackling issues of poverty. They have also began to adopt a similar attitude in their SHGs, with women's SHGs setting an example for the entire community.

Cooperative activities of SHGs have also benefited the community in more tangible ways. These activities included construction of approach roads to bring public transport to the village, construction and operation of day care centres, local school classrooms and cleaning of irrigation tanks and canals. The dynamism of the SHGs, reflected in these community-wide activities has helped defuse social conflict as the women's groups are seen to be bringing benefits to the entire community. The empowered scheduled castes have started to question, though mildly, caste differentiation.

The SHGs not only alleviate poverty in a temporary way, but also have the potential to eradicate it by tackling the root causes and processes that reproduce poverty intergenerational. Along these lines, the women members of SHGs have formed separate young-girls SHGs to mobilize their daughters, started night education and skill training classes for child labourers, or in some instances stopped child labour, used some of the loans for reproductive health and fertility control, (in some areas) formed agricultural unions to secure the legal minimum wages and challenged gender gaps in wages, and have begun resisting child marriages that they identify as one of the root causes of destitution and women's social subordination. In this sense, SHGs rather than being coping mechanisms represent a transformatory potential for the eradication of poverty.

The benefits of the project for women, indicated above, can be summarized as follows.

- The formation of groups has provided the women with confidence and a network of solidarity to tackle issues of poverty and (gender, class and caste-based) social discrimination that confront them.
- The SHGs, through the generation of savings habit in the community, mobilized community savings and made for easy availability of loans, facilities that did not exist earlier.
- The availability of consumption and emergency loans from their own savings has released the women from subservience to money lenders and gave them back their self dignity.
- The project created opportunities for women for income generation through access to credit and skill formation, by contributing to family welfare and increasing their status in the family.
- Group activities by the women for social action and community infrastructure have enhanced their status and respect in the community.

CONCLUDING REMARKS

The challenge is how to enable poor women particularly, as well as men, to get out of the energy-poverty trap, and have affordable and sustainable modern energy services. The main lesson is that for energy services to be affordable by poor women and men, it has to be for end-uses, which are directly productive and income generating. It is this chain of conversion of energy for income, which can facilitate the transition over time to cleaner, more efficient fuels, and more opportunities for enhancing productive and welfare uses of human time and energy. However the following outlook should facilitate in integrating gender-energy-poverty concerns in developing economies.

- Some 1.6 billion people, one-quarter of the world population have no access to electricity. In the absence of vigorous new policies, 1.4 billion people will still lack electricity in 2030.
- Four out of five people without electricity live in rural areas of the developing world, mainly in South Asia and sub-Saharan Africa. But the pattern of electricity deprivation is set to change, because 95 per cent of the increase in population in the next three decades will occur in urban areas.
- Some 2.4 billion people rely on traditional biomass namely, wood, agricultural residues and dung for cooking and heating. That number will increase to 2.6 billion by 2030. In developing countries, biomass use will still represent over half of residential energy consumption at the end of the outlook period.
- Lack of electricity and heavy reliance on traditional biomass are hallmarks of poverty in developing countries. Lack of electricity exacerbates poverty and contributes to its perpetuation, as it precludes most industrial activities and the jobs they create.
- Investment will need to focus on various energy sources, including biomass, for thermal and mechanical applications to bring productive, income-generating activities to developing countries. Electrification and access to modern energy services do not *per se* guarantee poverty alleviation.
- Renewable energy technologies such as solar, wind and biomass may be cost-effective options for specific off-grid applications, while conventional fuels and established technologies are likely to be preferred for on-grid capacity expansion.

REFERENCES

Chambers, R. (1996), *Whose Reality Counts?* IT Publications, London.

Kabeer, N. (1996), Agency, Well-being and Inequality: Reflections on Gender Dimensions of Poverty, *IDS Bulletin*, 27 (1): 11–21.

Moser, C.O.M. (1996), *Confronting Crisis: A Comparative Study of Household Responses to Poverty and Vulnerability in Four Poor Urban Communities,* Environmentally Sustainable Development Series and Monograph Series No. 8, World Bank, Washington, DC.

Sarkar, S. (2004), Air Pollution: Its Perilous Chronic Hygienic Impacts, *J Hum Ecol*, 16(2): 129-132.

Sarkar, S. (2005a), Poverty and Girl Child Labour: A Study in Brick Kilns, *South Asian Journal of Human Rights*, 1(1-2): 173-183.

Sarkar, S. (2005b), Economic Valuation and Health Linkages to Air Pollution, *International Journal of Environment and Development*, 2(2): 141-151.

Smith, K.R. (1987), *Biofuels, Air Pollution and Health: A Global Review*, Plenum Press, New York.

Sen, A. (1990), Gender and Cooperative Conflict, In: Irene Tinker (ed.), *Persistent Inequalities,* Oxford University Press, Oxford.

UNDP (1990), *Human Development Report*, Oxford University Press, New York.

UNDP (1997), *Human Development Report*, Oxford University Press, New York.

Chapter - 3

Air Pollution and Vulnerability

INTRODUCTION

The particulate concentrations and exposures are high in rural indoor areas in developing countries. It has been estimated that approximately half the global population and up to 90 per cent of rural households in developing countries still rely on biomass fuels (World Resource Institute 1999) and about 75 per cent of Indian households use biofuels for cooking and heating such as wood, agricultural residues and dung. Mothers and their children spend an average of six hours per day in highly polluted indoor areas. When households advance economically, they inevitably move up the energy ladder and eventually 'graduate' to the cleaner burning, more efficient fossil fuels; but poor economic conditions in developing countries and the rise in kerosene prices have limited the ability of populations to make this climb. Indoor air pollution affects women and small children far more than it affects any other sector of society. In developing countries cooking is the preserve of women. This means that of all family members they have the greatest exposure to indoor air pollution. Women typically spend between three and seven hours per day by the fire, longer when fires are also used for heating the home. Children under the age of five are also particularly at risk because they spend most of their time with their mothers; often very young ones are strapped to their mother's body. The impact this length of exposure has on small children is exacerbated by a number of factors. Children's airways are smaller, therefore more susceptible to inflammation. Their lungs are not fully developed until they are teenagers, so they breathe faster. Also, their immune systems are not fully developed a process that may be further delayed by malnutrition. These facts mean that children absorb pollutants more readily than adults and also retain them in their system for longer. Indoor air quality and indoor air pollutants are currently recognized as a potential source of health risks to exposed populations throughout the developing world. There is also increasing recognition that indoor air quality problems are strikingly different between developed and developing nations. The most significant issue that concerns indoor air quality in household environments of developing countries is that of exposure to emissions from combustion of fuels, particularly those used for cooking and heating. Women and children in developing countries are exposed to particulates in both ambient and indoor air in rural and urban settings. Particulates in ambient air, which emerge from a variety of sources, pose a serious problem. However, indoor air pollution (IAP) is a far more prevalent problem. Indoors, particulates are produced from tobacco smoke and the combustion of biomass fuels for cooking and heating. Environmental tobacco smoke is associated with acute respiratory infections (ARI) among women and children in developed countries, but fewer studies have documented this association in developing countries. In part, this may be because fewer studies have been conducted in the developing countries, but it also may be because smoking patterns are different in the developing world, children may spend less time in environments where smoking occurs, fewer women smoke (although this number is growing), and they may smoke fewer cigarettes per day etc. The most significant source of particulates appears to be combustion indoors of unprocessed solid fuel such as biomass and coal. Here the evidence of a reasonably strong relationship to acute respiratory infections among women and children is convincing and consistent. In fact, there is a reasonably good case for believing this relationship is causal, although the lack of any direct exposure measures in most studies and the difficulty of taking account of associated (confounding) factors mean there is some uncertainty about the evidence. IAP is a major risk factor, accounting for about 4 per cent of the global burden of disease measured by disability-adjusted life years lost. The acute respiratory infection among children below five years of age is 86 per cent in India and at global level it is also single largest disease category (Sarkar 2005). It is caused by the use of low-cost, widely available traditional energy sources such as coal and biomass such as wood, dung cake, crop residues etc. for cooking and home heating. Biomass is still the main source of energy for 60 to 90 per cent of households in developing countries, about 3.5 billion people. The health burden from IAP is greater in high-altitude rural areas and amongst poor families who tend to use cheap biomass and low quality coal fuels in primitive stoves without proper ventilation. Women and young children are at greatest risk because their gender roles and household responsibilities and behaviours, cooking and spending a lot of time indoors, result in high exposure to IAP (85 per cent of all global particulate exposure occurs indoors). Hence valuation of environmental quality improvements is required for the evaluation of environmental policy changes, and the estimation of environmentally corrected net national product. Environmental policy instruments and institutions including market contribute to the changes in environmental quality, the quality of water resources, atmosphere, forest and land. The choice of instruments and institutions for managing the environment requires the evaluation of environmental changes brought by them. One could identify three stages in a comprehensive method of valuation of environmental changes. In the first stage, a biophysical relationship between the environmental policy instrument and the environmental quality has to be established. The policy instruments considered could be the formal regulation by government using command and controls, pollution taxes, and marketable permits, the informal regulation by people's participation and the market management. The market management may result in the negative change in environment while the other instruments are designed to bring positive changes. In the second stage, a relationship between the environmental quality changes and the supply of environmental services like health, recreation, waste disposal, bio-diversity, climatic changes, and the sustainable livelihood for poor has to be found. In the third stage, a monetary valuation of environmental services has to be attempted. Thus the measurement of environmental values requires an interdisciplinary approach. It is the job of environmental scientists, engineers and ecologists in the first two stages to identify and estimate the relationship between policy changes and the environmental quality and the relationship between the environmental quality changes and the environmental services. The monetary valuation in the third stage has to be done by the economists. There could be a role played by social scientists in the first two stages also if the behavioural responses of polluters (in controlling pollution) and the users of environment (in minimizing damages from pollution) to the environmental policy changes are taken into account. The problem of particulate matter indoor pollution in India has been well documented (Smith *et al.* 1994; United Nation Environmental Program and World Health Organization 1992). Energy intensification has made air pollution a growing problem in many developing countries. Currently, policy researchers and decision makers believe that vehicles, industries and cooking with biofuels are the main contributors to this problem. Some of highest concentrations of air pollutants come about due to the use of biofuels for cooking in rural indoor environment (Sarkar 2004). In an attempt to set priorities for action, researchers have attempted to apportion the emissions of particulate matter across various sources (Bose 1990; Tata Energy Research Institute 1992), at various spatial scales. The limitations of such inventory-based exercises are that they completely ignore the role of meteorology (which determines the actual ambient concentration), the specific populations at risk and their behaviour (which determines the actual exposure). Individual exposure is a function of the concentration and the duration that the individual experiences it. There are many points at which air pollution might be measured and controlled. The best choice depends on the health-effects of concern, the relevant environmental pathways, and the resources available. In reality, health effects are not solely dependent on emissions and concentrations. Several studies of air pollution epidemiology have applied the statistical relationship between air pollution and human health outside the countries of the original studies, transferring dose-response coefficients (Pearce 1996). These studies attempting to value the economic benefits of air pollution control have demonstrated that intervening to reduce emissions can have significant health benefits, especially if health criteria use to choose as cost-effective interventions. While supporting this viewpoint, facilitating improvements in the indoor air environment will lead to even more significant health benefits being enjoyed by rural folk and slum dwellers, women and children below 5 years of age.

ECONOMIC VALUATION

The general approach of valuation is widespread to various methods of valuation developed in the literature. These methods are classified as physical linkage methods and behavioural linkage methods. In the physical linkage methods, the dose response functions described in the first two stages of valuation are estimated and the monetary valuation of changes in environmental services is made. For example, in the case of effect of environmental changes on human health (morbidity and mortality effects), the monetary valuation is made using the measures like the value of statistical life, and the disability adjusted life years. In the case of behavioural methods, the responses of various economic agents to the environmental policy changes are taken in to account. For example, in stage one the effect of policy change on the environmental quality depends on the behavioural response of polluters to the policy change. In the second stage, the effect of environmental quality changes on the environmental services depends on the behavioural responses of users of those services. The health effects of air or water pollution depend upon the mitigating and averting activities of people to minimize health damages. Finally the monetary valuation of environmental services depends on the people's perception of environmental values.

Various methods to measure benefits from environmental resources differ in their data requirements and the assumptions about economic agents and physical environments. The physical linkage methods assume that there is some sort of technological relationship between the environmental good and the user. The technological relationship can be either engineering or biological. These methods are also called damage function or dose response function approaches meant for measuring the effects of deterioration of air or water quality using market prices. The behavioural linkage methods on the other hand based on behavioural linkages between a change in the supply of environmental good and its effects. In these methods, the measurement of damages or benefits from a change in the supply of environmental good depends on the behavioural responses of users in the observed or hypothetical situations.

The behavioural linkage methods are classified as observed behavioural methods and the hypothetical behavioural methods. In the case of observed behavioural methods, measurement of benefits or damages from a change in the supply of environmental good is made making use of information related to the behavioural responses of users either in a simulated market for the environmental good or in the markets for private goods the demand for which depends upon the demand for the environmental good. In the case of hypothetical methods, individual values of environmental good are elicited in the hypothetical market like scenarios created through survey methods. The observed behavioural methods are the household production function models and the hedonic prices methods while the hypothetical behavioural methods are the contingent valuation methods. The observed behavioural methods use data from the real markets, the markets for the private goods which are complements or substitutes for environmental goods, to estimate the environmental values. It could be possible to make more reliable estimates of environmental values using observed behavioural methods. Hypothetical behavioural methods use data from the hypothetical markets created for environmental goods through survey instruments and therefore there could be uncertainties about the quality of data collected. There are at present a number of empirical studies using the household production models or observed behavioural methods for estimating the benefits from the improved urban ecosystems such as air quality, water supply and sanitation and tree cover in the developed countries. Given that there are not many similar studies available in the developing countries context, environmental policy changes in the developing countries are evaluated using a benefit transfer method, a method of using the models estimated for the developed countries for making the predictions about the benefits from the policy changes. The benefit transfer method may result in the under or over estimation of benefits from the environmental policy changes because the behavioural responses of households in the developed countries could be different from those in developing countries for a given environmental policy change. This difference in the behavioural responses could be attributed to differences in socio-economic characteristics and other attributes of households. It is therefore important to undertake a number of studies to estimate household production models using the developing countries data to obtain the accurate estimates of benefits from the environmental quality changes in these countries.

Recent empirical studies show that the observed behavioural methods of valuation could be used successfully to estimate the benefits from environmental quality improvements. These methods have the advantage of using data from the real markets for the commodities that are either substitutes or complements to environmental services. The required data could be obtained from the secondary sources or through household surveys. On the other hand the criticism of hypothetical behavioural methods or contingent valuation methods is well known and the empirical studies using these methods show that there could be lot of uncertainties about the quality of data obtained in the hypothetical markets for environmental services created through the survey methods.

Methodology of integrated environmental and economic accounting requires the development of physical and monetary accounts as satellite accounts to the conventional national income accounts. In case of environmental resources like air, the physical accounts help to identify the extent of degradation in relation to their natural assimilative capacity or carrying capacity. The supply of environmental services like the waste disposal services is fixed by the assimilative capacity of environmental media. The degradation of the resource takes place if the demand for its services exceeds its supply. The cost of environmental degradation in the measurement of environmentally corrected net national product (ENP) could be accounted in two ways. One method is to estimate the cost of improving the environmental quality from the current level to the quality corresponding to the natural assimilative capacity and deduct it from the estimate of conventional net national product (NNP). Another method is to estimate the user benefits or damages to households avoided in the hypothetical scenario of improving the environmental quality from its current level to the safe level or natural regenerative level and deducts this amount from NNP.

With a view to estimating the damages from air pollution a benefit transfer method can be used for this purpose. The parametric estimates of hedonic property prices model estimated using the pooled are used for making extrapolations. Damages to local households in selected study area from the pollution levels exceeding the safe level have to be accounted for in the estimation of environmentally corrected net national product (ENNP). Expenditures incurred by the households in the form of extra premium paid for houses in less polluted localities to avoid damages from air pollution form part of final consumption in the conventional national accounts. In an hypothetical situation of having air pollution at safe level in the selected study area, these expenditures would have not been incurred by the households. Therefore, estimation of ENNP requires the deduction of these expenditures from NNP estimated using conventional national accounts. Damages to local households in selected study area from the pollution levels exceeding the safe level have to be accounted for in the estimation of ENNP. Expenditures incurred by the households in the form of extra premium paid for houses in less polluted localities to avoid damages from air pollution form part of final consumption in the conventional national accounts. In a hypothetical situation of having air pollution at safe level in the selected study area, these expenditures would have not been incurred by the households. Therefore, estimation of

ENNP requires the deduction of these expenditures from NNP estimated using conventional national accounts. Damages from air pollution to all local households in a selected study area could be estimated given an estimate of number of households and the estimate of annual welfare gain to a typical household in the locality.

HEALTH LINKAGES

Smoke from the combustion of biofuels contains a large number of potentially hazardous pollutants. Exposure to these pollutants, especially suspended particular matter, is a risk factor for a wide range of diseases, including acute respiratory infections ARI, chronic obstructive pulmonary disorder (COPD), cancers, cataract and low birth weight. Research to date has not established reliable functions linking biomass fuel emissions to pollution concentrations, exposures, and health damages for households that rely on biomass fuels and traditional stoves. Based on a number of studies in developing countries, however, it appears that young children in households that use solid biomass fuels are 2-3 times more likely to suffer ARI than children in households that use other fuels. Similarly, women who have cooked over biomass fires for fifteen years are 2-4 times more likely to develop COPD than are other women (Smith 1999).

IAP is a major risk factor, accounting for 4 per cent of the global burden of disease measured by disability-adjusted life years (DALYs) lost. As a consequence, global ill health from air pollution may well be dominated by the effects of indoor exposure in developing countries (Table 1). It is caused by the use of low-cost, widely available traditional energy sources such as coal and biofuel for cooking and home heating. Biofuel is still the main source of energy for 60 to 90 per cent of households in developing countries, about 3.5 billion people. The health burden from IAP is greatest in high altitude rural areas and amongst poor families who tend to use cheap biofuels and low quality coal fuels in primitive stoves without proper ventilation. Women and young children are at greatest risk because their gender roles and household responsibilities and behaviours, cooking and spending a lot of time indoors, result in high exposure to IAP (85 per cent of all global particulate exposure occurs indoors). While acute exposure to smoke may result in carbon monoxide poisoning and death, most of the effects occur as a result of long-term exposure. There is strong evidence that chronic exposure to indoor air pollutants increases the risk of a range of respiratory illnesses, including acute lower respiratory infections (ALRI) in children and chronic obstructive pulmonary disease (COPD) in adults.

Table 1
Indoor Area Monitoring for Particulates in Biofuel Using Households in Developing Countries

Region (number of studies)	*Number of households*	*Duration of studies*	*Particulate level (micrograms per cubic metre)*
Pacific (2)	15	12 hr	1,300-5,200
South Asia (7)	504	Cooking	4,00-21,00
	135	Cooking	850-4,500(I)
	100	Non cooking	630-820
	68	Non cooking	880 (I)
	61	24 hr	2,000-2,800 (I)
China (8)	73	Various	2,600-2,900
	35	Various	1,100-11,000(I)
Africa (5)	28	Cooking/heating	800-1,700
	40	Cooking/heating	1,300 (I)
	100	24 hr	1,300-2,100 (I)
Latin America	42	Cooking/heating	440-1,100 (I)
and Caribbean	53	24 hr	340 (R)
(5)			720-1,220 (I)
			520-870 (R)

Source: Smith [1999].
Notes: Total number of studies is 27 and total number of households is about 600. I denotes inhalable and R stands for respirable.

In addition, chronic exposure to coal smoke results in increased risk for lung cancer. About 36 per cent of ALRI, 22 per cent of COPD and 1.5 per cent of cancers of the trachea, lung and bronchus are caused by exposure to IAP. Other conditions attributed to IAP for which the evidence is emerging but still inconclusive include increased susceptibility to asthma and middle ear infections in children, and tuberculosis, cataracts, and cancers of the nasopharynx and larynx in adults. Two studies have also implicated indoor air pollution in low birth weight and perinatal mortality. Finally, one could include burns (although not directly related to IAP), eye irritation, and fluorosis due to exposure to smoke from coal with high fluoride content through inhalation and ingestion. Several reviews have tried to estimate the global burden due to use of solid fuels by applying disease-specific relative risks or odds ratios to global estimates of the number of households using solid fuels. World Health Report 2002 finds that 2.7 per cent of the total global burden of ill health measured as DALY's is attributable to IAP, almost 80 per cent of which occurs in Africa and South East Asia. Indoor Air Pollution ranks eighth globally among risk factors, and fourth in developing countries with high morality, which make up 40 per cent of the world population, after under weight, unsafe safe and unsafe water, sanitation and hygiene, but before micronutrient deficiencies and tobacco. COPD and lung cancer are the main causes of death associated with IAP in China whereas ARI account for more than 80 per cent of the deaths and DALYs lost in India (Bruce *et al.* 2000; World Health Organization 2002).

Posing a serious health threat to women and children in developing countries is the burning of household fuels. India currently bears the largest number of IAP related health problems in the world, with 75 per cent of its households burning wood, dung, and crop residues. An estimated 500,000 women and children die in India each year due to IAP related causes which is 25 per cent of estimated IAP related deaths worldwide. The total estimates for premature deaths in Figure 1 ranged from 410,000 to 560,000 per year, with a best single estimate of 500,000. This accepts the full range of estimated risks for ARI, COPD, and lung cancer, calculated from odds ratios and background disease rates, and the low end of the range for the other conditions listed in Figure 1. Lung cancer and asthma related to indoor air pollution result in only a few hundred deaths. Indian women, who are largely nonsmokers and non-coal users, have low lung cancer rates. Deaths from indoor air pollution are distributed roughly as ARI 71 per cent, cardiovascular disease (CVD) 12 per cent, tuberculosis 12 per cent and COPD 5 per cent. The estimates imply that these causes account for 4 to 6 per cent of all deaths in India and for 7 to 9 per cent of deaths among women and children below 5 years. Addressing this health challenge is a massive task, with traditional biofuels accounting for more than 50 per cent of India's total energy supply, and more than 80 per cent of household energy supply. Women from poor families, in particular, suffer from severe health problems due to extended exposure to biomass smoke while cooking with traditional stoves, regularly inhaling large quantities of harmful pollutants.

Exposure to biomass smoke increases the risk of ARI in children less than five years of age. Children in The Gambia found riding on their mothers' backs as they cooked over smoky cook stoves were six times more likely to develop ARI than unexposed children. Similar studies in Nepal and Tanzania found dramatic increase in incidence of childhood ARI related to the time spent near a cook stove. Studies in India, Nepal and Papua New Guinea show that nonsmoking women who have cooked on biomass stoves for many years exhibit a higher prevalence of chronic lung disease. In Mexico, women exposed to wood smoke for many years faced 75 times more risk of acquiring chronic lung disease, about the level of risk that heavy cigarette smokers' face, than women not exposed to wood smoke. Exposure to high indoor smoke levels has been linked to pregnancy-related problems such as stillbirths and low birth weight in studies in Latin America, Asia, and Africa. It has also been associated with blindness (attributed to 18 per cent of cases in India) and immune system depression.

Figure 1
Diseases Linked to Indoor Pollution: Estimates for India

Diseases are listed by the strength of the evidence associating them with air pollution. The odds ratios cited are estimates from various studies. The odds estimate the rate of the disease or condition in a solid-fuel-using indoor environment compared with the rate in a non-solid-fuel-using environment. For each disease, estimates of annual excess premature deaths for India are given.

Strong Evidence

Acute respiratory infections (ARI). The largest single disease category worldwide (about one-twelfth of the global disease burden); accounts for about one-eighth of the disease burden in India. Odds ratio for young children: 2-3 (10 studies in developing countries). Premature deaths: 290,000-410,000.

Chronic obstructive pulmonary disease (COPD), such as chronic bronchitis. Accounts for about 1.5 per cent of deaths among Indian women. Odds ratio for women cooking over biomass fires for 15 years: 2-4 (4 studies in developing countries). Premature deaths: 19,000-34,000.

Lung cancer in women. Linked with cooking over open coal stoves in China; little evidence of a connection with biomass fuel. Odds ratio for more than 20 Chinese studies: 3ñ5. Premature deaths: 400-800.

Moderate Evidence

Blindness. Linked to use of biomass fuels for women in India, which has the largest burden of blindness of any region of the world.

Odds ratio for this group: 1.15-1.3. No premature deaths, but a significant burden of disability.

Tuberculosis. Odds ratio for Indian women: 1.5-3.0. TB is responsible for 5 per cent of the Indian burden of disease, a larger percentage than in any other region. Premature deaths: 50,000ñ130,000.

Perinatal effects (stillbirth; low birth weight; death or illness during the first two weeks after birth). Responsible for 8.8 per cent of the Indian burden of disease. Too little evidence to make estimates of premature deaths.

Suggestive Evidence

Cardiovascular diseases (CVD) and *asthma*. Known to be related to outdoor air pollution and passive smoking in industrial countries but does not seem to have been studied in developing-country households. Premature deaths: CVD, 50,000-190,000; asthma, 500-3,000 (based on urban air pollution studies, e.g., Ostro 1996).

Source: Smith [1998].

A large number of studies have attempted to estimate values of mortality risks, although usually in developed countries. These empirical estimates of the value of a statistical life (VOSL) are simply an extrapolation of an estimated willingness to pay for a marginal change in mortality risk. Table 2 summarizes some health valuation estimates from developing countries.

CONCLUDING REMARKS

The environmentally untenable economic development might result in the demand for ecological services exceeding the carrying capacity of ecosystems leading to their degradation. The air and water pollution and land degradation losing forest cover contribute to health damages, and direct utility losses to living being. These losses could be avoided by the environmentally sustainable planning at certain extra cost that could be less than the losses avoided. Methodically determined environmental standards are supposed to be determined by the carrying or natural regenerative capacity of environmental standard. Infringement of these standards in economic development could result in health and other damages to the human being. Benefit transfer method, a method of using the parameters of estimated models of environmental values in the developed countries to make estimates of environmental values in the developing

Table 2
Sample Value of Health Benefit

Country	*Value* [(a)(b)]	*Method*	*Source*
India	VOSL = $153,000-$358,000	Compensating wage differentials	Simon et al. (1999)
Pakistan	$67 to treat a case of severe, nonresistant bacterial pneumonia in a child under 5	Cost of medical treatment (clinic and hospital costs and pharmaceuticals only)	AMR Economics Working Group (2000)
Taiwan	$30.73 to avoid a 1-day episode of mild ARI, $52.01 to avoid a 5-day episode (not a cold)	Contingent valuation survey	Alberini et al. (1997)
China	VOSL = $45,547; RAD = $1.29	Benefits transfer	Florig (1993) in Pearce (1996)
Thailand (Bangkok) (1996)	VOSL = $336,000	Compensating wage differentials	World Bank (1994b) in Pearce
Indonesia (Jakarta)	VOSL = $75,000	Benefits transfer in Pearce (1996)	World Bank (1994a)
Egypt (Cairo)	VOSL = $62,021; RAD = $1.75	Benefits transfer	Chemonics International and Associates (1994) in Pearce (1996)
Mexico	(Mexico City) VOSL = $75,000	Human capital approach	Margulis (1992) in Pearce (1996)
Chile (Santiago)	RAD = $9.95	Value of a work day	World Bank (1994c) in Pearce (1996)

Source: Larsen and Rosen [2000].
(a) VOSL = Value of a Statistical Life
(b) RAD = Reduced Activity Day

countries is used to make estimates of damages from air and water pollution, and forest degradation in the developing countries. Such methods even though they provide over or underestimate of damages or benefits are justified on the grounds that the data are not available to estimate environmental values in the developing countries. The same logic of benefits transfer method could be used for making use of the parameters of household health production function model estimated using the pooled data. The estimate of health damages from air pollution, if could be obtained, might be taken as the part of cost of environmentally unsustainable economic development. This cost along with the damages from water pollution, and land degradation has to be deducted from the NNP estimated using conventional methods of national accounting to arrive at the environmentally corrected NNP. Environmentally corrected net national product for air pollution, could be estimated by deducting either the damages of air pollution or the cost of air pollution abatement for reducing pollution from the current level to safe level from the NNP estimated using the conventional methods of national income accounting.

REFERENCES

Alberini, A. et al. (1997), Valuing Health Effects of Air Pollution in Developing Countries: The Case of Taiwan, *Journal of Environmental Economics and Management*, 34: 107-126.

AMR Economics Working Group (2000), *The Costs of Antimicrobial Resistance: A Case Study of Childhood Pneumonia in Pakistan*, Harvard Institute for International Development.

Bruce, N., Perez-Padilla, R. and Albalak, R. (2000), Indoor Air Pollution in Developing Countries: A Major Environmental and Public Health Challenge, *Bulletin of the World Health Organization*, 78(9): 1078-1092.

Bose, R.K. (1990), *A Linear Goal Programming Model for Urban Energy-Economy-Environment Interaction in the City of Delhi*, Unpublished Ph.D Thesis, Indian Institute of Technology, New Delhi.

Chemonics International and Associates (1994), *Comparing Environmental Health Risks in Cairo, Egypt*, Report to USAID/Egypt.

Florig, H.K. (1993), *The Benefits of Air pollution Reduction in China*, Resources for the Future, Washington, DC.

Larson, B.A. and Rosen, S. (2000), *Household Benefits and Indoor Air Pollution Control in Developing Countries*, Prepared for the USAID/WHO Global Technical Consultation on the Health Impacts of Indoor Air Pollution and Household Energy in Developing Countries, Washington, DC.

Margulis, S. (1992), *Back of the Envelope Estimates of Environmental Damage Costs in Mexico*, World Bank Working Paper WPS 824.

Ostro,B.(1996), *A Methodology for Estimating Air Pollution Health Effects*, WHO/EHG/96.5, World Health Organization, Geneva.

Pearce, D. (1996), Economic Valuation and Health Damage from Air Pollution in the Developing World, *Energy Policy*, 24(7): 627-630.

Sarkar,S.(2004), Air Pollution: Its Perilous Chronic Hygienic Impacts, *Journal of Human Ecology*, 16(2): 129-132.

Sarkar,S.(2005), Natural Resource Environment, Pollution and Women health, In T. Sabanna, ed., *WTO and the Agriculture,* Serials Publications, New Delhi.

Simon, N. B. *et al.* (1999), *Valuing Morality Reductions in India: A Study of Compensating Wage Differentials*. World Bank, Washington, DC.

Smith, K.R, Apte, M.G, Yoqing, M, Wongsekiarttirat, W and Kulkarni, A. (1994), Air Pollution and the Energy Ladder in Asian Cities, *Energy*, 19(5): 587-600.

Smith, K.R. (1998), *Indoor Air Pollution in India: National Health Impacts and the Cost-Effectiveness of Intervention*, Indira Gandhi Institute for Development Research, Mumbai.

Smith, K.R. (1999), *Indoor Air Pollution*, Pollution Management In Focus Discussion Note Number 4, World Bank, Washington, DC.

Tata Energy Research Institute (1992), *Environmental Considerations in Energy Development: India Country Study,* Final report submitted to Asian Development Bank, Tata Energy Research Institute, New Delhi.

United Nation Environmental Program and World Health Organization (1992), *Urban Air Pollution in Mega Cities of the World,* Blackwell, Oxford.

World Bank (1994a), *Indonesia Environment and Development: Challenges for the Future*, World Bank, Washington, DC.

World Bank (1994b), *Thailand: Mitigating Pollution and Congestion Impacts in a High Growth Economy*, World Bank, Washington, DC.

World Bank (1994c), *Chile: Managing Environmental Problems-Economic Analysis of Selected Issues*, World Bank, Washington, DC.

World Health Organization (2002), *Reducing Risks, Promoting Healthy Life,* World Health Report, Geneva.

World Resource Institute (1999), *1998-99 World Resources: A Guide to the Global Environment,* Oxford University Press.

Chapter - 4

Biofuel and Health Linkages

INTRODUCTION

The concentration of indoor air pollutants coming out from combustion of biofuels such as wood, agriculture crops and dung cake used by rural households in developing countries cause severe health problems especially to women and children below five years. It has been estimated that approximately half the global population and up to 90 per cent of rural households in developing countries still rely on biomass fuels (World Resource Institute 1999) and about 75 per cent of Indian households use biofuels for cooking purposes. Typically cooked indoors in open fires or poorly functioning stoves, which leads to levels of air pollution that are among the highest ever measured. Therefore indoor air pollution with biofuels is an issue that requires to be addressed through gender, energy, environment and health policy. Some of highest concentrations of pollutants come about due to the use of biofuels for cooking in rural indoor environment (Sarkar 2004 a). In developed countries transformation has without exception been come with by a shift from biofuel to petroleum products (kerosene, LPG) and electricity. In developing countries even where cleaner more sophisticated fuels are available, households often continue to use biomass (Smith 1987). Although the portion of global energy derived from biofuel has fallen substantially which is evidence that biofuel use is increasing among the poor. Poverty is one of the main hurdles to the adoption of cleaner fuels and slow pace of development in many countries implies that biofuels will continue to be used by the poor for many years. Despite the magnitude of the problem of indoor air pollution, the health impact of this environmental exposure has been relatively neglected by research and policy makers.

Biofuels, being an important traditional source of energy, has developed a burly context. It has been showed that nearly 2 million people across the world struggle to meet their basic needs without access to affordable and adequate energy services. In sixteen countries in South and South East Asia over 2 billion people rely on biofuel for cooking, space heating and agro-processing (United Nations 2000). Its crucial importance to sustaining social life, food and nutrition and production activities has supported various national governments to focus heavily on the production and management of biofuel resources. Biofuel refers to any plants or animal based material deliberately burned by human beings. Wood is the most common biofuel, but use of animal dung and crop residues is also wide spread (De Koning *et al.* 1985). Some countries, including China and South Africa also use coal extensively for domestic needs. The types of fuels used typically amplify in cleanliness, convenience, efficiency and cost as people move up what has been termed the energy ladder (Figure 1). Animal dung is on the lowest rung of the ladder progressing to crop residues, wood, charcoal, kerosene, gas, and finally electricity. People generally move up the ladder as socio-economic conditions improve. Other sources of indoor air pollution in developing countries include smoke entering the home from nearby houses (Smith *et al.*1994), burning of forests, agricultural land and household waste, the use of kerosene lamps (McCracken and Smith 1998), and industrial and vehicle pollution. Environmental tobacco smoke is another source of indoor air pollution exposures, which can be expected to increase in importance in developing countries. It is important also to recognize that the open hearth and resulting smoke often have considerable cultural and practical value in the home, including control of insects lighting, drying food, fuel and housing materials and for flavouring foods (Smith 1987). The need to encompass biofuel for food and nutritional security has recently been reorganized and the provision of this essential need from production sources to consumption units, mostly households and the process of converting raw biomass into consumable energy are related to overall development. The implications of this process for the physical and psychological well being of the population or the total well being of those who are engaged in this development paradigm are central to sustainability. Their access to production sources, authority over production, modes of transportation and technology and also a nutritionally adequate diet to bear their daily workload

Figure 1
The Energy Ladder

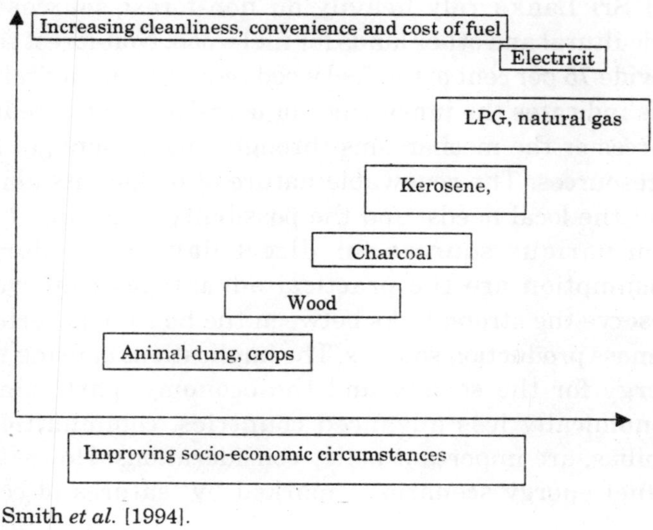

Source: Smith *et al.* [1994].

are crucial aspects. From these perspectives what is fundamental is the social domain within which a clear distinction between men's and women's responsibilities, work, social power and authority over resources and technology has been traditionally established. Their biological differences have been instrumental in the gender differentiation of their responsibilities in the biomass cycle. On this basis, the labour performed by women in the promotion of subsistence and well being has been separated from the work performed by men for cash and income. Similarly mostly in economically backward areas and communities, health repercussions are separated from energy systems and also from the benefits of using biomass as matters pertaining to women's ecology. Biofuel is composed of various portions of plants, including woody stems, barks, roots, twigs, and leaves, which can be burned in raw form to generate energy and it is used primarily by two sectors, wood energy based industries and the household sector, where it is used as a primary source of cooking energy. In South Asia the share of biofuel in the total energy consumption remains high, except in India (Table 1). These countries namely, Bangladesh, India, Pakistan, Nepal and Sri Lanka rely heavily on non-forest sources or on agricultural and other lands for fuel wood. Non-forest sources provide 75 per cent of the fuel wood requirement in Sri Lanka. This indicates the importance of users' access to production sources or the mechanisms through which users get access to resources. The renewable nature of biofuel, its ability to meet the local needs, and the possibility of getting it freely from various sources for direct day to day domestic consumption are the practical advantages that work to preserve the strong links between the household sector and biomass production sources. The implications of using biofuel energy for the society and the economy, particularly of economically less advanced countries, communities and families, are important policy considerations. However, the biofuel energy scenario is marked by features of concern common to many developing countries (Wickramasinghe 2003).

- The first is that biofuel still remains a dirty, messy, unhealthy fuel. Its use is very time consuming and undervalued and dominated by women, and it is used by a majority in developing countries.
- The second is that the unmeasured human costs in terms of human energy, time, discomfort, and personal health are paid mostly by the providers of this basic need from the multiple sources of supply to the household units of consumption.

Table 1
Fuel Wood Consumption in Some South Asian Countries

Country	*Total fuel wood consumption (Mt)*	*Share of forest wood (%)*	*Share of non forest wood (%)*	*Share of biofuel in total energy consumption (%)*
Bangladesh	5.5	13	87	71
India	94.5	26-53	43-74	33
Nepal	11.3	66	34	92
Pakistan	29.0	10	90	46
Sri Lanka	9.1	25	75	55

Source: Bhattarai [1996].

- The third is that the contributions made by women to sustain biomass energy systems are reckoned solely in the domestic domain, especially as a matter pertaining to domestic cooking, rather than as contributions towards maintaining human capital and quality of life.
- The fourth is related to the underreported realities of psychological trauma and the physical exhaustion of those whose lives are trapped in the biofuel cycle.
- The fifth is that the health risks of procuring and transporting biofuel are on the increase because of many changes in the supply domain, including resource tenure,

deforestation, degradation, market demand and competition for better quality wood and the burden of poverty and malnutrition experienced by women in particular.

In the developing economies a substantial share of employment is indeed in informal category and women in all age groups depend on the informal sector more heavily than men. Women are over represented in this sector in the sense that their share in the sector is higher than their share in total labour force. Most women tend to be own account workers and only a few are heads of micro enterprises. Relatively lower level of education among women, compared to men, seems to explain, in part, this gender differential in informal employment. Discrimination in the labour market also explains in part the disproportionate concentration as it limits women's access to formal and wage employment. Women also face additional constraints because of their homemaking and childcare responsibilities, which limits their participation in formal employment. Even within the informal sector more women than men seem to be in poor quality employment. In Latin America more women seem to be in the unpaid categories than men. In Africa the proportion of unpaid workers working in family owned enterprises among women appears to be relatively high compared to other regions. The causes for participation in the informal sector can be economic and non-economic. Economic reasons are related to unemployment and an inflexible formal labour market, a declining real price of capital and the high cost of formal production. Besides, non-economic causes are concerned with a greater flexibility and satisfaction in work, a complete use of workers professional qualifications and increased leisure time. There are two groups of factors, which determine the decision to become active in the informal sector, more specifically, the structural as well as opportunity factors. The structural factors consist of financial pressure, socio-psychological pressure and institutional constraints. The opportunity factors consist of individual background, skills, education, living condition or non-individual components, environment, values, standards etc. (Sarkar 2004 b). Unlike modern fuels, the supply of biofuels such as wood and charcoal are still largely uncontrolled and based in the informal sector. Rural populations generally supply themselves from surrounding forests and from trees in the landscape, in most cases in quantities that do not exceed sustainability limits. The supply of biomass fuel for the cities is also uncontrolled and in most cases, biomass production is unsustainable. Wood is felled in state-owned forests by dealers, but the cost of replacing the trees is not paid, with the result that forests are deteriorating rapidly around major cities. Past efforts to relieve the resulting firewood shortage by encouraging farmers to grow trees have largely failed because the costs of this far exceed the short term costs of gathering fuel from existing forests (French 1986). However new efforts to empower local communities to manage the forests in their areas in a sustainable way for the production, among other things, of biomass fuels are encouraging, particularly as this could provide income sources for the poor within the community. In most developing countries the majority of informal sector enterprises are owned and operated by women, with women making up the largest proportion of the work force. Despite this, the contribution of women entrepreneurs to national economies is not explicit in national statistics, leading to the development of policies that do not deal with the specific barriers faced by women linked to their gender-defined roles. Their enterprises tend to be concentrated in a relatively narrow range of activities such as knitting, dressmaking, crocheting, cane work and retail trading. These activities tend to have disproportionately low rates of return compared to the activities undertaken by men. However despite the low financial returns, women's enterprises provide important sources of household income, even in male-headed households. Women headed enterprises are frequently located in the home and these cottage industries tend to be overlooked by agencies because they are in the informal sector, which is diffuse and difficult to reach. When women are forced to close their enterprises, it is often for non-business reasons and linked to factors associated with working from home. The low rates of return prevent inward investment, hindering innovation and expansion, which are regarded as key factors in enterprise sustainability (Grosh and Somolekae 1996). There is little research to explain what forces drive these startups and shutdowns, and how gender influences these processes. Women's access to resources (such as credit, land and education, which are recognized as key factors in micro enterprise development) is significantly less than that of men. Generally, research in small and medium-scale enterprise sustainability indicates that a lack of working capital is one of the two most common causes of enterprise failure (Grosh and Somolekae 1996). Women's access to decision-making within the household and community is also restricted, reducing their ability to influence processes and resource allocation. Given the disproportionate number of poor women in rural areas, research which takes into account gender aspects of the transformation of structures and processes could make a significant contribution to the development of gender equitable sustainable livelihoods. The role of energy in the sustainability of women's enterprises is also not well understood. In food processing enterprises it has been estimated that energy costs are 20 to 25 per cent of the total inputs, which would suggest that technological interventions could increase the scale and profitability of these businesses. Figure 2 gives some examples of how energy can act as an opportunity or a constraint on women's productive activities. The types of enterprises that women are traditionally involved in are energy intensive and rely on biomass fuels. Even in rural areas, women may have to buy fuel wood to run enterprises such as beer making (McCall 2001). An important issue is what sort of mechanisms can assist women in gaining access to improved energy services. Grain mills, which are very popular with women, since they improve product quality as well as reducing women's labour, are typically only provided by the private sector, and are still absent in many rural locations. A much more systematic approach is needed, possibly with some form of incentive to encourage the spread of mills to areas not yet served. A general rule that can be learnt from attempts to introduce technology for women is that if it does not reduce the labour in household tasks then, no matter how beneficial the technology, it is likely to have low acceptance. There are positive examples of women taking up energy technologies that have contributed to increasing their incomes. It is found those women's groups in Ghana use LPG for fish preservation, giving them a better quality product than when using wood, and enabling them to reach export standards, considerably improving their income (Mensah 2001). Women may in fact be best entrants to become energy entrepreneurs. It has indicated that improved stove programmes in India run by women tend to be rather successful because they are able to more easily approach their clients (Sarin 1984). However energy entrepreneurship could extend beyond stoves to include energy services, for example the supply of and even the repair of, modern energy appliances such as solar panels. There is an enormous need for agents in rural areas who can distribute such equipment on a viable basis, notwithstanding with some support in the short term. Women who live in rural areas know and understand local circumstances and needs and may have a much clearer idea about the energy services that rural people desire. In addition a woman may be able to sell more effectively to other women, since access to female clients is not hindered by social constraints. This may in fact be the best route to greater women's participation in household energy choice.

Figure 2
Energy in Livelihood Strategies: Improving the Position of Women

Energy availability that creates opportunities (increased income/more sustainable use of natural resources)

- Community level sustainable management of forests can provide income through organized firewood production and sale.
- Energy entrepreneurship as a secondary activity for community service and income generation.
- Improved technologies for charcoal production can boost sustainability and incomes.
- Availability of mechanical and process heat technologies can be a stimulus to the start up of various small-scale enterprises (sawing, food processing etc.).

Energy scarcity as a constraint (which if removed, can bolster other activities, reduce vulnerability, improve food security, increase well being).

- Lack of transport for moving harvest products to storage and to market may be a disincentive to produce (increases vulnerability, and reduces food security).
- Poor cooking technology results in unnecessary ill health for women and children reducing their productivity (and threatening well being).
- Lack of cheap, easily available, fuel forces women to spend large amounts of time gathering fuel, and restricts the boiling of water and in some cases the adequate cooking of food resulting in ill health (threatens well being, increases vulnerability) as well as limiting time available for other enterprises.

REVIEW OF LITERATURE

Air pollution has been consistently linked with substantial burden of ill health in developed and developing countries (Bruce *et al.* 2000; Schwartz 1994; Smith *et al.* 2000). The bulk of indoor air pollution research and control has focused on sources of concern in developed countries based on solid fuel and tobacco combustion (Smith and Mehta 2003). Exposures to indoor air pollution are of importance cause of morbidity and mortality in developed countries (World Health Organization 1997, 2002) as well as developing countries (Florig 1997; Saksena and Dayal 1997; World Bank 1997; World Health Organization 1997). However the most important indoor air pollutants are the combustion products of unprocessed solid biomass used by the vulnerable section urban and rural people in developing countries for cooking and heating purpose. Exposure to biomass smoke enhances the risk of acute respiratory infection among women and children below five years. A study in Gambia focuses that infants who were exposed to smoke by being carried on their mother's backs during cooking were nearly three times more likely to develop significant cases of acute respiratory infection. A study in Colombia expresses that women cooking over open fires had almost four times more chronic lung disease compared to those cooking in other manner (Parikh 1996). A study in Tanzania finds that children younger than five years who died of acute respiratory infection were almost three times more likely to be sleeping in a room with an open cook stove than healthy children in same age group. Studies in India, Nepal and Papua New Guinea show that non-smoking women who have cooked on biomass stoves for many years exhibit a higher prevalence of chronic lung disease. In Mexico, women exposed to wood smoke for many years faced 75 times more risk of acquiring chronic lung disease, about the level of risk that heavy cigarette smokers face than women not exposed to wood smoke. A recent study in Colombia discloses that women exposed to smoke during cooking were three times more likely to suffer from chronic lung diseases. A study in Japan delves into high rates of cancer among women who had previously used wood as fuel. The risk of lung cancer is high in Chinese women exposed to coal smoke in homes. Likewise a study in Africa encompasses that cooking with wood greatly increased the risk of stillbirth.

Considerable amount of carbon monoxide have been detected in the bloodstream of women cooking with biomass in India and Guatemala (World Bank 2000). It has been estimated that about half a million women and child die each year from air pollution in India. Compared to other countries India has among the largest burden of disease due to the use of dirty household fuels and 28 per cent of all death due to indoor air pollution in developing countries occurs in India (Smith, 2000a). It is estimated that use of open fires with biofuels exposes nearly 2 billion people in the world to enhanced concentrations of particulate matter and gases, up to 10-20 times higher than health-based guideline values available for typical urban outdoor concentrations (Barnes *et al.* 1994; Reddy *et al.* 1996; World Health Organization 1999). Assessments of the burden of disease attributable to use of biofuels use in India have put the figure at 3-5 per cent of the national burden of disease (Smith 2000b; Smith and Mehta 2003). Some of the earliest human evidence linking indoor air pollution from biomass combustion with respiratory health came from studies carried out in Nepal and India (Pandey 1984a; Ramakrishna *et al.* 1989; Smith *et al.* 1983). Since then, there has been a steady stream of studies, especially on women who cook with these fuels and young children (Bruce *et al.* 2000; Smith *et al.* 2000). Associations between exposure to indoor air pollution and increased incidence of chronic bronchitis in women and acute respiratory infections in children have been documented (Armstrong and Campbell 1991; Bruce *et al.* 1998; Ezzati and Kammen 2001; Robin *et al.* 1996). Many recent studies have also been conducted in rural Indian villages (Awasthi *et al.* 1996; Behera *et al.* 1991; Mishra and Retherford 1997; Smith 1993; Smith 1996). A recent study has also characterized the exposure response relationship between biomass smoke exposure and acute respiratory infection in children of rural Kenyan households (Ezzati *et al.* 2000a). The incidence of chronic obstructive pulmonary disease in non-smoking women using biomass for cooking has also been shown to be dependent on the number of years cooking with biofuels and often to be comparable to that of men who usually have high smoking rates. Based on this evidence, it has been estimated that the indoor air pollution contributes to 3-5 per cent other causes as well, it is difficult, lengthy, and of the national burden of disease in India (Smith 2000b).

Exposure to indoor air pollution, especially to particulate matter, from the combustion of biofuels has been implicated as a causal agent of respiratory diseases in developing countries (Chen *et al.* 1990; Ellegard 1996; Pandey 1984b). This association, coupled with the fact that globally more than 2 billion people rely on biomass as the primary source of domestic energy, has put preventive measures to reduce exposure to indoor air pollution high on the agenda of international development and public health organizations (Ezzati *et al.* 2000b; World Bank 1993). The evaluation of the benefits and effectiveness of measures that aim to reduce these negative health impacts, such as design and dissemination of improved stoves and fuels, requires knowledge of the exposure response relationship between indoor particulate matter from biomass combustion and acute respiratory infections. There is little information on the shape of the exposure response relationship at concentrations of hundreds to thousands of micrograms per cubic meter that are commonly observed in indoor environments in developing countries (Ezzati *et al.* 2000b).

The epidemiological studies have provided some evidence of an association between cataract or blindness and exposure to indoor smoke from household use of solid biofuels fuels such as animal dung, wood and crop residues (Mishra *et al.* 1999; Zodpey and Ughade 1999). However, these studies have had limitations that have precluded establishment of a definitive causal relationship. The study of Zodpey and Ughade (1999) found an association between cataract and cheaper cooking fuels such as coal, cow dung and wood presented limited data on potential confounding factors, other than age and socioeconomic status. The other study, with a cross sectional design, used data from the 1992-93 Indian National Family Health Survey which found an association between biomass fuel use and partial and complete blindness after adjustment for a number of potentially confounding factors (Mishra *et al.* 1999). Use of biofuels causes a number of respiratory problems, which include acute respiratory infections in children, chronic obstructive lung disease in nonsmokers (Samet *et al.* 1987). It has also been implicated as a risk factor for lung cancer in women (Gao 1996; Wu and Du 1996).

OBJECTIVE AND METHODOLOGY

Rural women have often been ignored in policies to enhanced access of the poor to more efficient and convenient forms of energy in developing countries including India. Rural development programmes have therefore had limited success in alleviating air pollution, including the drudgery of fuel wood collection and biomass based cooking that cause danger to the health of rural women and children. The challenge has to be addressed in a broader perspective including social and behavioural aspect. A community cooking with biofuels can be exposed to several health diseases and to alleviate such problem gender participation promotion may be an appropriate solution. The highest concentration of indoor air pollutants emerges from burning of biofuels such as wood, agriculture crops and dung cake, which are widely used by rural households in rural North Bengal. Compared to the thousand of studies outdoor air pollution in developed country urban settings, only a handful of studies nearly a few dozen have been carried out in biomass using households in developing countries, most of which are rural settings. The different characteristics of fuel uses such as major fuel used for cooking time and effort involved in getting that particular fuel and availability of other type of fuels in the area, cooking practices, exposure to indoor pollution, health impact along with socio-economic conditions of households in rural villages especially women in rural North Bengal can be comprehended from the study. The pollutants released due to use of biofuels for cooking need to pay more attention to the mass rural women living daily with exposure to indoor air pollutants and to curb indoor air pollutants exposure to acceptable level access of clean fuels is required for the better health of rural women. Policies for rural areas that encourage the uptake of efficient use of biomass fuels can effectively address the problem of indoor air pollution and physical drudgery of women. But women must involve in the planning of these policies and interventions to ensure their successful implementation and sustainability. Energy policies and projects by themselves will not change the plight of women in the society, but these can be used as entry point for reducing a preventable burden of death and illness among women and promoting greater fairness in the allocation of opportunities and resources between men and women.

The present study on indoor air pollution and women health in the informal sector of rural North Bengal is purely based on primary data using survey research technique. There is a definite need for better and comprehensive household energy survey in rural areas in developing countries with a view to better understanding the current and changing pattern of fuel use over time and to ensure women participation in planning and execution of programmes targeting indoor air pollution and build up their awareness towards health, environment and energy issues. The study strongly purports to seek interdisciplinary relevance with issue relating to gender studies, health economics, energy and environment perspective. The different characteristics of fuel uses such as major fuel used for cooking time and effort involved in getting that particular fuel and availability of other type of fuels in the study area, cooking practices, exposure to indoor air pollution, health impact along with socio-economic conditions of households in rural villages of North Bengal especially women engaged in informal activities and children below five years of age can be comprehended from the study. However the major objective of the study includes the following:

- Socio-economic status of the households.
- Fuel use pattern and cooking practices of the households.
- Reasons for not using clean fuel and willingness to pay for it.
- Association among combustion of biofuels, air pollution and women health.

The selection of villages from rural North Bengal for the purpose of extensive survey was carried out using multistage sampling method. At primary stage stratification of the regions was done on the basis of socio-cultural districts. At the second stage selection of one district per socio-cultural districts was done based on the population median class. At the third stage allocation of households to each district based on the universe of rural households was undertaken. Then stratification of each selected district was done by village population size. The villages were categorized into four different strata on the basis of population. In stratum I villages with population less than 1500 were included; stratum II had villages with population 1500-3500, whereas in stratum III villages with population between 3500-5500 were included. In stratum IV villages with population more than 5500 were considered. Stratum IV was excluded from the sample because these villages resemble semi urban areas. The selection of the villages from each stratum was done using population proportion sampling and selection of households within the selected villages was performed based on systematic random sampling. The survey was carried out at household level including individual responses for health status, village level as well as local health care facility. Village level and health centre surveys were performed for the sake of validation of data acquired at household and individual level. At the household level a multi pronged approach was used while collecting different types of information. Data were collected through face-to-face interview of the chief cook of the house along with any helping hands and health status was assessed with the help of qualified medical practitioners. Various socio-economic information and other details as well as individual self-reported data were gathered through structure questionnaire survey. The information collected for the study comprise of socio-economic characteristics, fuel consumption pattern, cooking behaviour along with health profile.

The survey was conducted in rural villages of Cooch Behar, Darjeeling, Jalpaiguri, and Malda districts covering 2,580 individuals, of which 967 women, 1,082 men, 255 girls and 276 boys below 14 years in 740 households in 20 villages. The sample respondents were selected using stratified random sampling techniques from the surveyed villages. The village level information was collected from the head of village *panchayat* whereas health centre level information was gathered from administrative officer or chief doctor. The data at household level were congregated to get a comprehensive picture of socio-economic conditions, energy use pattern, cooking behaviour, willingness to pay to curb indoor air pollution and health considerations.

FINDINGS

In rural North Bengal most of the people are engaged in the informal sector, of which women are generally employed in domestic services, *beedi* making, agriculture and allied activities, construction work, brick making and rural artisans. It is observed that most of the surveyed villages are linked with road network and have some mode of transportation. In the selected villages 13 villages have *pucca* road within a kilometre distance and other 2 villages have pucca road within 2 kilometres distance and 5 villages have pucca road beyond 2 kilometres but less than 4 kilometres distance. Only 2 villages have railway station within a distance of 3 to 6 kilometres and people in rest of the 18 villages face difficulties to avail railway transportation because of locating station at long distance. Most of the villages (60 per cent) have a town within a distance of 2 to 5 kilometres. As the majority of the surveyed villages are close to pucca roads, the main mode of transportation is bus. Add to there is other modes of transportation such as van rickshaw and bicycle. Almost all villages have at least a primary school and 7 villages have secondary school also. 16 villages have primary health centres with an average distance of 2 to 4 kilometres.

Economic compulsion is the main reasons of the women behind taking the job as informal workers (98 per cent). However there is a tiny percentage (2 per cent) of the workers mostly the wives from middle class families, who entered the informal job market for passing out idle time. Besides child labourers entered the workforce for meeting their own educational expenses. 16.96 per cent of women workers reported that they have chosen the job for supporting their family and 29.68 per cent of the workers serve for independent income. It is also reported that most of the adult male members of the households are agriculture workers (62.01 per cent). Others engage as casual labour (5.53 per cent), rickshaw puller (9.89 per cent), petty trader (7.76 per cent), wholesale trader (3.79 per cent) and government employee (1.02 per cent). It is found that 10 per cent among them do not work at all.

The women do simultaneously their own household task. They combine wage work with their domestic responsibilities. Table 2 discloses the level of participation in own household task as reported by female members of the households.

Therefore women including girl children have nearly full responsibilities in activities such as washing clothes and utensils, water collection, fuel collections, food preparation and childcare activities. Apart from the large bulk of sundry task often some workers are to assist their counterparts in agriculture activities. In addition girl children are to help their mother in sundry household task especially water collection, fuel collection and food preparation.

Table 2
Level of Participation in Own Household Task

Household task	*Self*	*Husband / Other members*	*Jointly*
Washing clothes and utensils	1043 (85.35)	57 (4.67)	122 (9.98)
Water collection	1117 (91.41)	32 (2.62)	73 (5.97)
Fuel collection	937 (76.68)	187 (15.30)	98 (8.02)
Food preparation	1222 (100.00)	0 (0)	0 (0)
Maintenance of house	482 (39.44)	527 (43.13)	213 (17.43)
Childcare	1098 (89.85)	83 (6.79)	41 (3.36)

Note: Figures in the parentheses are percentages and female members include girl children

The survey shows that 52.3 per cent of the households have annual income less than Rs. 25,000 while 35.54 per cent of the households have annual income above Rs. 25,000 but below Rs. 50,000. only 7.16 per cent of the households have income more than Rs. 50,000 but below Rs. 75,000.The different types of durables owned by the households reveal the purchasing power/economic status of the households. The survey discloses that majority of the households are unable to buy anything additional for the family. It is also found that female members of the households working for more than ten years failed to save sufficient amount of money to buy durables.

It is found that almost all (94.46 per cent) of surveyed households in rural villages North Bengal use biofuels for cooking. Among biofuels using households, 78.25 per cent use fuel wood. Dung cake and crop residue are used in 73.4 per cent and 35.48 per cent of households respectively. The average consumption of fuel wood is about 5.4 kgs per households, supplemented by other biofuel sources. Kerosene is mostly used for lighting and its use for cooking is restricted to only 5.68 per cent of the households. Only 14 households make use of LPG and use of electricity and biogas for cooking is almost trivial. The study reveals that most of the households cook (87.03 per cent) twice meals a day. 5.41 per cent of the households cook once. Remaining 7.57 per cent of the households cook thrice a day. The average time spent for cooking a day is about 4 hours along with other associate sundry household task.

Willingness to pay of the participants estimates the probable demand for kerosene. The kerosene supplied through public distribution system is mostly limited to quota. The study shows that most of the villages do not get kerosene through rationing system and 3 villages reported to have an irregular supply of kerosene. The use of clean fuel is higher among higher income group. Only 48.24 per cent of the households are drawing kerosene as per quota from ration shop. About 53.78 per cent of the households are to buy an average quantity of 8 litres kerosene per month for lighting and cooking from open market. The survey reveals that at the ration price almost all sampled households (99.05 per cent) are willing to purchase an additional quantity of kerosene. 62.03 per cent of the households are ready to switch over to clean fuel if made available. The results of the survey show that only 6.35 per cent of the households are willing to spend some money to improved air quality in the kitchen. There is a higher willingness to pay for ventilation in houses than for improved stoves.

The households not using kerosene for cooking are asked for the reasons for not using clean fuels. 83.67 per cent of the households reported non-availability as the reason for not using it, while 69.78 per cent do not use clean fuels because of non-affordability. 17.91 per cent are not interested to switch over to clean fuel and a tiny percentage of households agree with other reasons (Table 3).

Table 3
Reasons for not using Clean Fuels

Reasons	*Percentage agree*
Lack of availability	83.67
Costly	69.78
Not willing to switch over	17.91
Anxious of using	23.93
Taste of food changes	78.52
Not persuaded of the advantages	8.31
Wood smoke repels for insects	1.58
Wood smoke enhances the longevity of thatched roof	3.3
Base: household not using kerosene for cooking	698

The air pollution has been consistently associated with substantial burdens of ill health in developed and developing countries. The study of selected villages reveals that women and children are badly affected by pollution. It is found that most of the diseases are indoor air such as bronchitis, tuberculosis, asthma, eye disease, adverse pregnancy outcomes, skin infection, joint pain, other respiratory diseases etc. Also general muscular weakness, phlegm and cough among children have been noticed in the villages. A majority of complaints are about problems regarding bronchitis and tuberculosis. The women suffering from respiratory diseases are 46.4 per cent. Asthma was reported by 10.1 per cent whereas 4.8 per cent reported bronchitis. The reporting of symptoms and diseases were kept into account on the basis of respondent's memory recall for all the members of the households. Incidence of asthmatic symptoms noticed to be higher among women who cook inside compared to those who cook open air. On the basis of self reported symptomatic cases of respiratory diseases cough, breathlessness, wheezing are found to be significantly higher among those living *kachcha* houses and using biofuels for cooking compared to those living *pucca* houses and using clean fuels for cooking.

CONCLUDING REMARKS

Indoor air pollution comes out to be a major environmental and public health hazard for large numbers of the world's poorest, most disadvantaged people. The existing studies on indoor air pollution in developing countries, while providing important evidence of associations with a range of serious and common health problems, suffer from a number of methodological limitations. There is also a strong case for carrying out a limited number of intervention studies, particularly for the most common and serious health outcomes from indoor air pollution due to burning of biofuels. Such studies may adopt a randomized controlled trial design, which will provide the most powerful evidence and remove the problem of confounding, or be based on natural experiments if appropriate settings are found. Case-control or cohort studies may also serve this purpose if suitable areas can be identified where a good range of exposure levels are distributed fairly evenly and confounding factors are not too strongly associated with exposure. The stress that future studies should shell out more attention to exposure assessment implies a need to further develop practical and valid methods for measuring the exposure levels and patterns particularly for women and children. However the following policy and strategy recommendations have been made.

- A general improvement in the health status especially that of women and children, is a critical input for economic growth and poverty reduction, thus addressing the health impacts of household energy and indoor air pollution should be an integral part of poverty reduction efforts.
- Improved biomass stoves and cleaner biomass based fuels will continue to be an option for reducing exposure for a large majority of the rural poor in developing countries. Facilitating behavioural changes in women, children and other household members is another way of reducing exposure and alleviating the associated health impacts.

Improving the status of women can be an effective method of promoting markets for better stoves and other household energy use services.

- The government should ensure sustained upshot market mechanisms for distribution of improved stoves and commercial fuels. Programmes that propagate improved biomass stoves with higher efficiency and lower emissions commercially, with proper certification and quality control by government agencies, have greater financial sustainability, respond better to user demand and produce more durable stoves. Therefore, government interventions should be re-oriented towards creating a effective regulatory framework and incentive structure that works with the market.
- One of the most important elements of a strategy to mitigate indoor air pollution is to bring about a behavioural change, including a greater demand for cleaner cooking. This will require raising awareness amongst rural households about the health impacts of traditional household energy use and providing specific information on the range and effectiveness of mitigation options.
- Among the rural poor, at the household level the decision making regarding fuel use patterns largely depend on men, while girls and women continue to put up with the burden of collecting fuel wood and use it for cooking, thus exposing themselves to highest levels of indoor air pollution. It is therefore important to ensure mechanisms that allow both women and men to make choices and influence household decisions regarding the use of fuels. Creating self-help groups, promoting energy entrepreneurship and ensuring income generation opportunities for women as part of household energy strategy are the approaches that may improve rural living standards.

- The effective household energy programmes should address the range of sustainable livelihood and poverty needs of both women and men. In poor households, energy and time use for consumption and production are closely interrelated such as food and beverages may be prepared for family use as well as for sale; fuel wood may be collected for cooking and for sale etc. Increasing opportunities for women to earn income outside of the household may be the only way to reduce the use of fuel wood collected with unpaid family labour and therefore engagement in paid informal activities may generate income for the rural women. Programmes to improve household energy services and mitigate indoor air pollution need to address these aspects, by providing opportunities for income earning for women engaged in the informal economic activities.

REFERENCES

Armstrong, J.R. and Campbell, H. (1991), Indoor Air Pollution and Lower Respiratory Infections in Young Gambian Children, *Int J. Epidemiol*, 20 (2): 424-429.

Awasthi, S., Glick, H. and Fletcher, R. (1996), Effect of Cooking Fuels on Respiratory Diseases in Preschool Children in Lucknow, India, *Am. J. Trop. Med. Hyg.*, 55 (1): 48-51.

Barnes, D.F., Openshaw, K., Smith, K.R. and Van der Plas, R. (1994), *What Makes People Cook with Improved Biomass Stoves? A Comparative International Review of Stove Programs,* World Bank Technical Paper, Energy Series 242, Washington DC.

Behera, D., Jindal, S.K. and Malhotra, H.S. (1991), Ventilatory Function in Nonsmoking Rural Indian Women Using Different Cooking Fuels, *Thorax*, 46 (5): 344-346.

Bhattarai, T.N. (1996), *Integrating Wood Fuel Production in the Implementation of Agriculture, Forestry and Rural Extension Programmes in South Asia,* Regional Wood Energy Development Programme in Asia, Report No. 26, Food and Agriculture Organization, Bangkok.

Bruce, N. (2000), *Global Technical Consultation on the Health Impacts of Indoor Air Pollution and Household Energy in Developing Countries,* USAID/WHO, Washington, DC.

Bruce, N., Perez-Padilla, R. and Albalak, R. (2000), Indoor Air Pollution in Developing Countries: A Major Environmental and Public Health Challenge for New Millennium, *Bulletin of the World Health Organization*, 78(9): 1078-1092.

Chen, B.H., Hong, C.J., Pandey, M.R. and Smith K.R. (1990), Indoor Air Pollution in Developing Countries,*World Health Stat Q*, 43:127-138.

De Koning, H.W., Smith, K.R. and Last, J.M. (1985), Biomass Fuel Combustion and Health, *Bulletin of the World Health Organization*, 63(1): 11-26.

Ellegard, A. (1996), Cooking Fuel Smoke and Respiratory Symptoms among Women in Low-Income Areas in Maputo, *Environ Health Perspect*, 104: 980-985.

Ezzati, M., Saleh, H. and Kammen, D.M. (2000a), The Contributions of Emissions and Spatial Microenvironments to Exposure to Indoor Air Pollution from Biomass Combustion in Kenya, *Environ Health Perspect*, 108: 833-839.

Ezzati, M., Mbinda, B.M. and Kammen, D.M. (2000b), Comparison of Emissions and Residential Exposure from Traditional and Improved Biofuel Stoves in Rural Kenya, *Environ Sci Tech.*, 34:578-583.

Ezzati, M. and Kammen, D.M. (2001), Quantifying the Effects of Exposure to Indoor Air Pollution from Biomass Combustion on Acute Respiratory Infections in Developing Countries, *Env Health Perspect*, 109:481-489.

Florig, H.K. (1997), China's Air Pollution Risks, *Environ Sci. Tech.*, 31(6): 276A-279A.

French, D. (1986), Confronting an Unsolvable Problem: Deforestation in Malawi, *World Development,* 14 (4): 531-540.

Gao, Y.T. (1996), Risk Factors for Lung Cancer among Nonsmokers with Emphasis on Lifestyle Factors, *Lung Cancer,* 14 (Supplementary 1): S39-S45.

Grosh, B and Somolekae, G. (1996), Mighty Oaks from Little Acorns: Can Micro Enterprise Serve as the Seedbed of Industrialization? *World Development,* 24 (12): 1879-1890.

McCall, M. (2001), Brewing Rural Beer should be a Hotter Issue, Boiling Point, 47: 23-25.

McCracken, J.P. and Smith, K.R. (1998), Emissions and Efficiency of Improved Wood Burning Cook Stoves in Highland Guatemala, *Environ Int,* 24(7): 739-747.

Menash, S.A. (2001), Energy for Rural Women's Enterprises, In: *Generating Opportunities: Case Studies on Energy and Women,* United Nations Development Programme, New York.

Mishra, V. and Rutherford, R. (1997), Cooking Smoke Increases the Risk of Acute Respiratory Infections in Children, *National Family Heath Survey Bulletin* (8).

Mishra, V.K., Retherford, R.D. and Smith, K.R. (1999), Biomass Cooking Fuels and Prevalence of Blindness in India, *J Environ Med*, 1:189-199.

Pandey, M.R. (1984a), Prevalence of Chronic Bronchitis in a Rural Community of the Hill Region of Nepal, *Thorax,* 39:331-336.

Pandey, M.R. (1984b), Domestic Smoke Pollution and Chronic Bronchitis in a Rural Community of the Hill Region of Nepal, *Thorax,* 39: 337-339.

Parik, J. (1996), *Poverty, Environment and Development Nexus*, Human Development Report. UNDP.

Ramakrishna, J., Durgaprasad, M.B. and Smith, K.R. (1989), Cooking in India: The Impact of Improved Stoves on Indoor Air Quality, *Environ Int*, 15: 341-352.

Reddy, A.K.N., Williams, R.H., Johansson, T.B. (1996), *Energy after Rio: Prospects and Challenges*, United Nations Publications, New York.

Robin, L.F., Lees, P.S.J., Winget, M., Steinhoff, M., Moulton, L.H., Santhosham, M. and Correa A. (1996), Wood Burning Stoves and Lower Respiratory Illness in Navajo Children, *Pediatr Infect Dis. J.*, 15: 859-865.

Saksena, S. and Dayal, V. (1997), Total Exposure as a Basis for the Economic Valuation of Air Pollution in India, *Energy Environment Monitor,* 13(2): 93-102.

Samet, J.M., Marbury, M.C. and Spengler, J.D. (1987), Health Effects and Source of Indoor Air Pollution, Part I. *Am Rev Respir Dis,* 136:1486-508.

Sarin, M. (1984), *Nada Chula: A Handbook,* Voluntary Health Association of India, Delhi.

Sarkar, S. (2004a), Air Pollution: Its Perilous Chronic Hygienic Impacts, *J. Hum. Ecol.,* 16(2): 129-132.

Sarkar, S. (2004b), Theorising in Informal Sector: Concept and Context, *Social Action,* 54(40): 359-373.

Schwartz, J. (1994), Air Pollution and Daily Mortality: A Review and Meta Analysis, *Environ Res.,* 64:36-52.

Smith, K.R., Aggarwal, A.L. and Dave, R.M. (1983), Air Pollution and Rural Biomass Fuels in Developing Countries: A Pilot Village Study in India and Implications for Research and Policy, *Atmos Environ,* 17: 2343-2362.

Smith, K.R. (1987), *Biofuels, Air Pollution, and Health. A Global Review,* Plenum Press, New York.

Smith, K.R. (1993), Fuel Combustion, Air Pollution and Health: The Situation in Developing Countries, *An Rev. Energy Env.,* 18: 529-566.

Smith, K.R., Apte, M.G., Yoqing, M., Wongsekiarttirat, W. and Kulkarni, A. (1994), Air Pollution and the Energy Ladder in Asian Cities, *Energy*, 19(5): 587-600.

Smith, K.R. (1996), *Indoor Air Pollution in Developing Countries: Growing Evidence of its Role in the Global Disease Burden*, Organizing Committee of the 7th International Conference on Indoor Air Quality and Climate, Seec IshibashiI Inc., Japan.

Smith, K.R. (2000a), Indoor Air Pollution Implicated in Alarming Health Problems, In: *Indoor Air Pollution-Energy and Health for the Poor*, Newsletter Published by World Bank.

Smith, K.R. (2000b), The National Burden of Disease in India from Indoor Air Pollution, *Proc Nat Acad Sci.*, 97: 13286-13293.

Smith, K.R., Samet, J.M., Romieu, I. and Bruce, N. (2000), Indoor Air Pollution in Developing Countries and Acute Lower Respiratory Infections in Children, *Thorax*, 55:518-532.

Smith, K.R. and Mehta, S. (2003), The Burden of Disease from Indoor Air Pollution in Developing Countries: Compared of Estimates, *Int. J. Hyg. Environ Health*, 206:279-289.

United Nations (2000), *World Energy Assessment: The Challenge of Sustainability*, United Nations, New York.

Wickramasinghe, A. (2003), Gender and Health Issues in the Biomass Energy Cycle: Impediments to Sustainable Development, *Energy for Sustainable Development*, VII (3): 51-61.

World Bank (1993), *Investing in Health*, World Development Report, Oxford University Press, New York.

World Bank (1997), *Clean Water, Blue Skies: China's Environment in the New Century*, World Bank: 114, Washington, DC.

World Bank (2000), *Household Energy, Air Pollution and Health*, UNDP/ESMAP.

World Health Organization (1997), *Health and Environment in Sustainable Development,* Geneva.

World Health Organization (1999), *Guidelines for Air Quality*, Geneva.

World Health Organization (2002), *Reducing Risks, Promoting Healthy Life,* World Health Report, Geneva.

World Resource Institute (1999), *1998-99 World Resources: A Guide to the Global Environment,* Oxford University Press.

Wu, J.M and Du, Y. X. (1996), Overview and Highlights of the Panel Discussion, *Lung Cancer*, 14 (Supplementary 1): S3-S8.

Zodpey, S.P. and Ughade, S.N. (1999), Exposure to Cheaper Cooking Fuels and Risk of Age Related Cataract in Women, *Ind. J. Occupational Environ Med.*, 3:159-161.

Chapter - 5

Informalised Working Women

INTRODUCTION

The term informal sector was first used by Keith Hart (1970) in a study of urban Ghana and it has been further refined by International Labour Organization (ILO 1972) while studying the employment situation in Kenya. The informal sector is characterized by ease of entry, small-scale operations, family ownership of enterprise, labour intensive and adaptive technology, lack of support and recognition from the government, competitive and unregulated product market, unprotected labour market, undisclosed income or tax evasion etc. In addition to these, the other characteristics include deplorable working condition and low level of wage, low capital accumulation and reinvestment, insecure and temporary nature of employment etc. Besides, the informal sector may be classified into four categories on the basis of their nature of works namely, home based workers, self-employment workers, piece wageworkers and time wageworkers. The causes of informalisation may be of economic recession, evasion of tax as well as excessive governmental regulation of market sector.

The urban economy can be classified broadly as formal and informal sectors. As far as the contrasting characteristics of the two sectors are concerned, the entry into the informal sector labour market is unrestricted and level of earning is also very low, while that in formal sector labour market, entry is restricted and level of earning is high. Apart from the distinguishing characteristics, there exist strong direct and indirect inter-linkages between formal and informal sectors (Sarkar 2006a).

The employment in the informal economy has risen rapidly in all regions of the developing countries and various forms of non-standard employment have emerged in most regions of the developed countries. In the developing economy, it was only the once rapidly growing economies that experienced substantial growth of modern sector employment. However, in the wake of the recent economic crisis, most of these countries experienced a substantial decline in formal wage employment and a concomitant rise in informal employment. How many retrenched workers have been reinstated in formal jobs as these economies have begun to recover from the crisis is not yet known. Why has the informal economy continued to expand and grow? There is no simple answer to this question as different causal factors are at work in different contexts. However, some mix of the following sets of factors would explain the persistence or expansion of the informal economy in most countries, regions, or industries. The first set of factors relates to the pattern of economic growth. Some countries have experienced little or no economic growth, while others have pursued capital-intensive growth or what some observers call jobless growth. In both such contexts, not enough jobs are created for all those seeking work. Many frustrated formal job seekers find employment or create their own work in the informal economy. Another pattern of economic growth namely high tech growth tends to create more high-skill service sector jobs than lower-skill manufacturing jobs. In such contexts, those without the skills to compete for high-tech formal jobs find work or continue to work in the informal economy. There is another, more optimistic, scenario namely, growth from below. In some countries the tiny business and micro-business sectors are more dynamic and create more jobs than the formal sector. The second set of factors has to do with economic restructuring and economic crisis. Available evidence suggests that during periods of economic adjustment whether due to economic reforms or economic crises, the informal economy tends to expand. This is because retrenched workers move into the informal economy when public enterprises are closed or the public sector is downsized. This is also because households need to supplement formal sector incomes with informal earnings in response to inflation or cutbacks in public services. The third set of factors relates to the globalization of the world economy. Global trade and investment patterns tend to privilege capital, especially companies that can move quickly and easily across borders and to disadvantage labour especially lower-skilled workers that cannot migrate easily or at all. To enhance their global competitiveness more and more investors are moving to countries that have low labour costs or shifting to informal employment arrangements. Furthermore, there has been a radical restructuring of production and distribution in many key industries characterized by outsourcing or subcontracting through global commodity chains. The net result is that more and more workers are being paid very low wages and many of them have to absorb the non-wage costs of production. Globalization also tends to privilege large companies who can capture new markets quickly and easily to the disadvantage of small and micro entrepreneurs who face difficulties gaining knowledge of much less access to emerging markets. In sum, globalization puts pressure on low-skilled workers and petty producers by weakening their bargaining power and subjecting them to increasing competition. Why should the persistence or expansion of the informal economy be of interest or concern? There is a link between working in the informal economy and being poor. Average incomes are lower in the informal economy than in the formal sector. As a result, a higher percentage of people working in the informal economy, relative to the formal sector, are poor. However, there is no simple relationship between working in the informal economy and being poor or working in the formal sector and escaping poverty (Sethuraman 1998; Thomas 1995). The relationship between informal employment and poverty appears only when informal workers are classified by employment status and by industry or trade. Informal incomes worldwide tend to decline as one move across the following types of employment from employer to self-employed to informal and casual wageworkers to industrial outworker. The link between working in the informal economy and being poor is stronger for women than for men. A higher percentage of women than men worldwide work in the informal economy. Moreover, there is a gender gap in incomes and wages in the informal economy. This is because women worldwide are under-represented in higher income employment statuses in the informal economy (employer and self-employed) and over represented in the lower income statuses (casual wage worker and industrial outworker). Available evidence suggests that globalization of the economy tends to reinforce the links between poverty, informality and gender. This is because global competition tends to encourage formal firms to shift formal wageworkers to informal employment arrangements without minimum wages, assured work, or benefits and to encourage informal units to shift workers from semi-permanent contracts without minimum wages or benefits to piece-rate or casual work arrangements without either assured work, minimum wages, or benefits. This is also because globalization often leads to shifts from secure self-employment to more precarious self-employment, as producers and traders lose their market niche. With these shifts, and as more and more men enter the informal economy, women tend to be pushed to the lowest income end of the informal economy. But globalization can also lead to new opportunities for those who work in the informal economy in the form of new jobs for wageworkers or new markets for the self-employed. However, a collaborative effort on the part of grassroots organizations of those who work in the informal economy with sympathetic representatives of non-governmental, research, government, private sector and international development organizations is needed to enable the most vulnerable segments of society to seize these opportunities. There needs to be a much more detailed interpretation of who is in the informal economy and what they are doing, as well as a more comprehensive analysis of how globalization, particularly trade and investment policies, are affecting the employment arrangements and income sources of those who work in the informal economy (Sarkar 2006b).

TAXONOMY OF TYPOLOGY

All informal activity has one common feature namely the entrepreneurs who works in the informal economy perceive the benefits of doing so to offset the costs of going formal. Recent studies have identified a number of reasons why some entrepreneurial activity may take place in the shadows. The most important determinants are the prevalence of burdensome and costly government regulations and the level and administrative complexity of taxation. Informality comes at a cost, the inability to use government and some private sector services available to firms that fully comply with regulations. In countries entrepreneurs may well opt to be formal, even if regulations are many and taxes are high. In contrast, entrepreneurs in countries where the quality of public services to enterprises is poor have a much easier choice. In the absence of discernible benefits of going formal, they prefer to save their time and money and stay informal. Many transition economies have experienced surging share of entrepreneurial activity in the informal sector. Some of this activity is illegal. Such activity will not become formal, regardless of improvements in the enterprises climate. Other activities, like small production units operate merely for the subsistence of their owners and do not generate enough revenue to make their inclusion in the tax base meaningful. However, there exists a considerable share of entrepreneurial activity that is semi-formal e.g., the organization is registered but most changes. Informal activities usually fall into three broad categories namely employees are not, and can become formal with appropriate policy underground enterprises, subsistence enterprises and unofficial enterprises.

Subsistence enterprises result from coping strategies adopted by families to compensate for low wages or external shocks e.g., unemployment etc. Unofficial enterprises generally result from the desire to escape or avoid the administrative and/or financial burden of regulation e.g., license and permit regimes, taxes, labour regulations etc. Firms around the world lie on a spectrum of entrepreneurial

Table 1
A Taxonomy of Typology of Informal Sector

	Informal sector	
	Subsistence enterprises	*Unofficial enterprises*
Degree of informality	100 per cent	High proportion of sales and workers not registered
Type of activity	Single street traders, cottage/micro enterprises, subsistence farmers	Small manufacturers, service providers, distributors, contractors
Technology	Labour intensive	Mostly labour intensive
Owner profile	Poor, low education, low level of skills	Poor and non-poor, well educated, high level of skills
Markets	Low barrier to entry, highly competitive, high product homogeneity	Low barrier to entry, highly competitive, some product differentiation
Finance needs	Working capital	Working capital, some investment capital, supplier credit
Other needs	Personal insurance, social protection	Personal perhaps business insurance

Source: Djankov et al.[2003].

activity, ranging from informal to formal. A typology of the informal sector is presented in Table 1. Another typology represents categories of informal work based on the context of the work. Informal work may involve a person working for someone else or a person being self-employed and within each of the categories there are two arrangements (Table 2).

Table 2
Structure of Informal Work Typology

	Primary work for firm	*Extra work for current employer*
Person works for someone else	Works off the books Works under the table Paid in cash and not taxed	Works extra hours on weekends or evening (paid in cash and not taxed)
	Person operate own tiny business	Does sporadic odd jobs, services or products
Person self employed	Cash only exchange Ongoing, regular Business is seen primary income May invest income into business	Works extra hours on weekends or evening (paid in cash and not taxed)

Source: ILO [2002].

Following the worker approach workers in the informal economy can be broadly distinguished into wage employment and non-wage employment, each consisting of the components of own account workers, employers/owners of informal enterprises with at least one hired worker; unpaid family helpers in both types of informal enterprises, employees in the enterprises of informal employers, outworkers or home workers (persons working at home, or on premises of his choice other than the employer's, to produce goods or services on a contract or order for a specific employer or contractor), independent wage workers not attached to only one employer and providing services to individuals, households and enterprises, e.g., domestic workers and watchmen working for households and informal employment in formal sector enterprises (workers whose pay and benefits do not conform to existing labour regulations). This categorization is similar to that developed by Sethuraman (1998). In the literature the first four categories are generally taken to represent employment in the informal sector. The need to distinguish the category of independent wageworkers can be debated. In many Latin American countries domestic helps are distinguished in the national surveys and together with independent wageworkers are added to the informal sector (Sethuraman 1998). The first process of informalisation of the labour force, pushing work out of formal work situations, leads to an increase in the first component, non-wage employment. It can also lead to increase in the first two varieties of the second component i.e., informal wage employment. The second process of informalisation, resulting in looser contracts and fewer benefits, leads to an increase in the last category of workers, informal employment within the formal enterprises as defined by the enterprise-based approach. Obviously it is not easy to obtain empirical estimates of these categories of workers from the national official labour statistics. However, an approximation of the first component of the informal economy can be arrived at, non-wage employment or self-employment, by the addition of employers, own account workers and unpaid family helpers in the activity status classification of the national labour force survey. While it may be relatively safe to assume that own account workers and unpaid family helpers are part of the informal economy, this assumption may not be very accurate for the category of employer. Employers, however, form a very small proportion of the workforce. The second component of the informal economy is even more difficult to demarcate from the official data since there is really a continuum in the degree of informality in the employer-employee relationships. The official data distinguish only employees. The Indian labour force surveys further classifies them into casual and regular. All regular workers do not necessarily belong to the formal economy, as they often do not receive a variety of benefits due to the formal worker such as provident funds, paid leave etc. An approximation of the second component of the informal economy can be made by assuming that all casual employees definitely constitute a part of the informal economy since they are least likely to obtain any of the benefits accruing to formal economy workers. Another indicator or measure of the nature of informality of the work status or sector is the earnings differentials. The informal economy can be distinguished by the inferior quality of work and inferior terms of employment, both remuneration and benefits. Among the non-wage component inferior technologies lead to low productivity and hence to low earnings or incomes.

Since informal sector is very diverse and it covers many types of work, so it is difficult to classify it into a specific group as uniform. However, the workers in the informal sector may be classified broadly into four categories as under:

Home Based Workers

The workers in this category carry out their activities using their traditional skill and labour. The majority of the home based workers work in the privacy of their homes and they are invisible. This category of workers engages in earthen pots making, rural artisans etc.

Self Employed or Own Account Workers

Self-employed or own account workers are those who do not have any permanent place for carrying out their activities. Some of them have to change their place of activity almost on a daily basis. In this category of workers includes street vendors, hawkers, rag pickers, rickshaw pullers, sex workers etc.

Piece Wage Workers

There has been a tremendous growth of private informal manufacturing such as garment making, knitting etc. These categories of workers are employed by entrepreneurs. They are usually employed on a piece rate basis. This type of workers carries out their work independently, but employers exercise control over them by supplying raw material and sometimes advancing minimum cash. This kind of labour is often found in beedi making, carpet and mat weaving, lace industry etc.

Time Wage Workers

This type of workers sells their labour power in exchange of a low paid time rate of wage. The most of the workers in this category are quasi permanent. These workers are placed in a most disadvantageous position. Their activities rely heavily on manual labour. This category includes gardeners, cleaners, sweepers, construction labourers, bricks workers, agricultural labourers, domestic helps etc.

SOCIAL SECURITY MEASURES

Social security is both a concept as well as a structure. It represents basically a system of protection of individuals who are in need of such protection by the State as an agent of the society. Such protection is relevant in contingencies such as retirement, resignation, retrenchment, death and disablement that are beyond the control of the individual members of the society. State as a representative of the society has an important mandate to keep parity with such differences through a protective cover to the poor, the deprived and the disadvantaged. The concept of social security is now generally understood as meaning protection provided by the society to its members through a series of public measures against the economic and social distress that otherwise is caused by the stoppage or substantial reduction of earnings resulting from sickness, maternity, employment injury, occupational diseases, unemployment, invalidity, old age and death. The ILO concept of social security is based on the recognition of the fundamental social right guaranteed by law to all human beings who live from their own labour and who find themselves unable to work temporarily or permanently for reasons beyond their control. At the international level, the preamble of the charter of ILO also referred to the need and protection of workers against sickness, disease and injury arising out of their employment, pension for old age, protection of the interests of the workers who were employed in countries other than their own. Thus the right to social security was recognized officially for the first time. Social security has been recognized as an instrument for social transformation and progress and must be preserved, supported and developed as such. Furthermore, far from being an obstacle to economic progress as is often alleged, social security organized on a firm and sound basis will promote progress, since once men and women benefit from increased security and are free from anxiety will become more productive. There is considerable controversy about the social and economic effects of social security and most of the current debate is focused on its supposedly negative effects. Social security is supposed to discourage people from working and saving to reduce international competitiveness and employment creation and to encourage people to pull out from the labour market prematurely. On the other hand, social security can also be observed to have a number of very positive economic effects. It can help to make people capable of earning an income and to increase their productive potential, it may help to maintain effective demand at the national level and it may help create conditions, in which a market economy can flourish, notably by encouraging workers to accept innovation and change. A formal social security system presupposes the interventionist role of the State on redistribution grounds. Social security measures are generally income, maintenance measures intended to provide a minimum living to the people when they are deprived of the same due to invalidity, unemployment or old age. The two basic elements of social security are provision of a minimum living to those who are deprived of the same and selective redistribution of income to a target group to reduce inequalities. Social security to the workers would involve providing or framing such schemes or services or facilities and amenities, which can enable the workers to lead a decent minimum standard of life and having economic security to fall back upon in the event of loosing job for whatsoever may be the reason in the circumstances beyond their control. The workers must be given the wages and other services, which will enable them and the members of their family to lead a decent life. Thus social security is an instrument for social transformation and good governance. Social security in India was traditionally the responsibility of the community in general. Currently ongoing measures towards transformation process has added a new dimension to the issue and enhanced the requirement further towards a planned and regulated institutionalized measure in the form of social security in its common understanding. Low-income women workers constitute one of the most vulnerable groups in Indian society. Their vulnerability arises from their irregular work, their low economic status, their little bargaining power, their lack of control over their earnings, their need to balance work with care for children and homework and their lack of assets. Unequal gender relations indeed assume an important role in defining their insecurities (Dasgupta 2003).

Social security comprises of two types of measures namely, promotional and protective. Promotional measures consist mainly of employment, training and nutrition schemes by which a person is able to work and earn a livelihood. Protective measures consist of schemes by which the State provides the means of livelihood when a person is not able to work (Subramanya 2000). ILO standards relating social security are mainly protective and have been designed primarily for the formal sector. There are many possible measures for social security provision for the informal sector, but two specific models have been explored as follows (Sarkar 2004).

Welfare funds represent one of the methods for providing social security to the workers in the informal sector in India. Welfare funds are of two types, namely, contributory and tax based. The funds set up by the central government are tax based, while those set up by the government of Kerala are mostly contributory. A contributory scheme is akin to social insurance. In India, there is only one social insurance scheme, namely, the employees' social insurance scheme. The funds may be administered departmentally or by autonomous body and are financed by the central as well as State governments. The other scheme, namely, the government of India's, tax based welfare funds cover mine workers, beedi rollers, cine workers and workers in building and construction industry. The fund is administered by the office of the director general, labour welfare, through its regional offices and financed by special levies in the forms of cess.

The State funds are mainly contributory based on contributions from employers, workers and government, and administered by labour departments of respective State governments. The funds cover wide range of facilities including health care, education for children, housing and water supply, old-age and survivor benefits, group insurance schemes and recreational facilities. The central welfare funds for mine workers and beedi rollers may be used for improvement of public health and sanitation, prevention of disease, and provision and improvement of medical facilities, water supplies and facilities for washing, educational facilities, standards of living including housing and nutrition, amelioration of social conditions and provision of recreational facilities, family welfare including family planning and other services. Although the model has been implementing successfully in India, still, mine and beedi workers have no provision for meeting the expenditure on any of the well recognized branches of social security like benefits of sickness, occupational injury, maternity, invalidity, old-age, survivor or unemployment.

Insurance corporations in India have been providing social insurance to the workers in the informal sector. With the assistance of Central and State governments, they have introduced various schemes, which are administered directly through government or more successfully through cooperatives and non-government organizations and are a combination of social assistance and social insurance. The Life Insurance Corporation (LIC) in India has developed group insurance, which is akin to social insurance based on large numbers. It has the potential to provide social security to those in the informal sector. The scheme offers life insurance cover at a premium of Rs. 10 for every Rs. 10,000 of benefits. Up to Rs. 5,000 coverage is subsidized up to 50 per cent by one time capital grant from the government. This model has been adopted by the central government, State governments and voluntary organizations to cover the life insurance of many groups of workers in the informal sector. The largest of these schemes, where the premium is contributed by the central government, is for landless agricultural workers. There are many other group insurance schemes for workers in the informal sector, for milk producers, handloom weavers, rickshaw pullers, shop assistants, sweepers, beedi workers, fish farmers and others. The scheme of the LIC provide mainly survivor benefits, some also provide old-age pensions too. Apart from the LIC, the General Insurance Corporation (GIC) of India also administers a few social security schemes such as personal accident social security scheme for poor families, the hut insurance scheme and the solatium fund. The GIC has also launched a health insurance scheme and has been monitoring the comprehensive group insurance scheme for the central government. The schemes of the GIC include invalidity benefits, health insurance and protection against loss of property.

Some other schemes of social security protection in the informal sector include:

- Childcare services to workingwomen, especially crèches for children of working mothers have been implemented by the Central Social Welfare Board.
- Under National Maternity Benefit Scheme, central assistance is provided in the form of payment of Rs.300 each to pregnant women for first two childbirths.
- Under Family Benefit Scheme, central assistance is given in the form of payment of a lump sum of Rs.5000 to families below the poverty line on the death of their breadwinner.
- Under National Old-age Pension Scheme, central assistance is extended to States for payment of old-age pension to men and women who have attained the age of 65 or more at Rs. 75 per month.
- Assistance in case of sickness, either in the form of a lump sum or reimbursement of medical expenses, assistance in case of death of bread winner and maternity assistance is provided by many voluntary organizations as well as co-operative societies.

Several State governments of India have taken initiatives to provide various protective social security measures for workers in the informal sector. A few States such as Andhra Pradesh, Gujarat, Kerala and Tamil Nadu also have special pension schemes for agricultural workers. Maternity benefits for landless agricultural labour have been introduced in Gujarat, Karnataka and Kerala to compensate loss of wage due to absence at work. However, health care as a part of the social security does not seem to exist in any State. Gujarat, Tamil Nadu and Kerala have certain welfare schemes exclusively for women and children while a number of other States offer welfare benefits for various categories of population below the poverty line.

Successive governments in Kerala have introduced a number of social security and welfare schemes in view of attaining the goal of minimizing income insecurity among the weaker sections. It has various schemes for the benefits of the informal sector (Rajan et al. 1999). The most important protective type schemes in terms of coverage are old-age pensions for destitute and rural labourers. Another innovative programme in Kerala is the creation of welfare funds. In order to meet the demands of the informal sector workers, some types of social insurance and other non-wage benefits, a new institutional innovation was come into limelight in the form of welfare funds. With the active support from the trade unions, the government of Kerala took the initiative to create a fund through contributions from worker, employers and government.

Apart from the Kerala, Tamil Nadu has been a pioneer in implementing social security protection for the workers in the informal sector (Guhan 1993). The main initiatives are liberalized pensions, accident relief scheme, new survivor benefit scheme, maternity assistance scheme and marriage grant scheme. It has been implementing protective social security for providing nutrition to vulnerable groups such as pregnant and destitute women and the aged and the like. Other States in India and developing countries can learn from the experiences of Kerala and Tamil Nadu on what can be done in the area of protective social security measures at reasonable cost to help the vulnerable groups. Some other States have also taken important initiatives in recent years, namely, employment guarantee scheme in Maharashtra, primary education in Himachal Pradesh and Madhya Pradesh, public distribution in Andhra Pradesh and land reform in West Bengal. In contrast, in States like Bihar, Uttar Pradesh, Rajasthan, there seems to be apathetic towards the necessity to build social security schemes (Mahendra Dev 2000).

A number of State governments have also set up welfare funds for various categories of workers. The government of Kerala has set up about 35 welfare funds for different categories of occupations and sectors. These welfare funds cater to the needs of agricultural workers, auto rickshaw workers, cashew workers, coir workers, construction workers, fishermen and women, handloom workers etc.

The government of Assam has set up a statutory fund under Assam Plantation Employees Welfare Fund Act, 1959 for the benefit of the plantation workers. Similar funds have also been set up in Gujarat and Maharashtra under Bombay Labour Welfare Fund Act, 1953 and in Karnataka under Mysore (Karnataka) Labour Welfare Act, 1965 and in Punjab under the Labour Welfare Act, 1965.

The State governments of Andhra Pradesh and Uttar Pradesh have also set up welfare funds for various categories of workers. All these welfare funds however, cater to a very small segment of the total workforce. In view of the change in the perception of the social security i.e., an essential input to the productivity rather than burden on exchequer, some State governments are making concerted efforts to extend social security to the workers in the informal sector. For instance, the government of Karnataka is going to set up a social security authority of Karnataka and create a welfare board to cater to the needs of the 66 identified occupational groups shortly. Further, occupational groups can be added to it as and when the necessity arises. The welfare fund will be created by levying a cess from transport vehicles, employer's contribution, workers and the State government when there is no employer. The fund created therein will be utilized to implement schemes and programmes covering pension, health, housing, insurance in case of death and disability aspects for the benefit of workers.

Recently, the government of West Bengal initiated State Assisted Scheme of Provident Fund for Unorganized Workers. The scheme covers all wage employed and self-employed workers between the ages of 18 to 55 years in the unorganized sector having an average family income of not more than Rs. 3500 per month. Each subscriber worker contributes a sum of Rs. 20 per month and equal matching amount contributed by the state government. The interest on the balance at credit of subscriber is also paid by the state government annually at the rate declared by the State government. Total contribution along with interest has to be refunded to the worker on attainment of the age of 55 years. The scheme will have provision for loans and withdrawals from the fund as prescribed by the State government. The government of West Bengal had identified 50 industries in the unorganized sector and 16 self-employed occupations, of which 13 unorganized industries and 7 self-employed occupations are being covered in the first phase. These industries include tailoring shops, establishments having less than 20 workers, bakery, handloom, construction, earthen pottery, stone crushing, auto repairing, etc. The self-employed occupations include cycle rickshaw, head load workers, railway/street hawkers, auto rickshaw operators, mason and cobblers.

The Department of Agriculture of the State of Punjab implements a scheme financed from the funds available with marketing committees/boards to provide financial assistance to the farmers and labourers in case of death or injury by operating the agricultural machinery/implements and undertaking other operations both at the level of farm since 1984. The scope of the scheme includes death or disablement to any farmer or labour working in the agricultural machinery implements or arising out of the use of the said machinery implements in the state of Punjab, death or disablement to any farmer or labour arising out of digging of tube-well in the State of Punjab or electric current while operating tube-well in the farm, death or disablement to any farmer or labour while using the insecticides or pesticides in the State of Punjab or due to snake biting while working in field or watering the field and death or disablement to labour employed in field arising out of use of agricultural machinery implements. The financial assistance provided under the scheme includes payment of Rs.75,000 in case of death, Rs. 30,000 in case of partial disability such as loss of one leg, eye, arm or serious injury, Rs. 45,000 in case a farmer or labour lost both eyes, arms, leg, etc. Rs. 7,500 to Rs. 22,500 in case of loss of fingers and Rs. 30,000 in case of loss of four fingers, which is treated as loss of one arm. The group was apprised of the free medical check up camps being organized by the government of Punjab. Workers working in hazardous and dangerous process establishments come in contact with various toxic substances and other chemicals from which they are likely to contact with occupational diseases. The government of Punjab has decided to carry out free medical check up of such workers. Till date 165 medical check up camps have been organized in which 50,000 workers have been examined and medicines worth Rs. 18 lakhs were spent in these camps by the employers which generated a lot of goodwill. 3500 workers were referred to hospitals for their blood test, chest X-rays, surgical operations, skin diseases, leprosy etc. This is a very welcome step in the right direction as it demonstrates the willingness of the State to share the burden in delivery of health services.

The government of Tamil Nadu introduced Tamil Nadu Social Security and Welfare Scheme-2001. These schemes cover manual worker, auto rickshaws and taxi drivers, washer-men, hairdressers, tailoring workers, handicraft workers and palm tree workers. The State government is planning to formulate scheme for handlooms and handloom silk-weaving workers, footwear and leather goods manufacturing and tannery workers and artists. State government has set up the goal and social security and welfare fund for the respective workers. Every worker registered under the scheme for two years initially has to pay a sum of Rs. 100 and every employer 3 per cent of the wages payable by him to the worker employed to the social security and welfare board. The fee for renewing the registration is Rs. 10. The funds are to be utilized for paying premium towards insurance coverage having provision of compensation of Rs. 1 lakh in case of death or loss of both hands, feet, Rs.50,000 in case of loss of one hand or one foot and Rs. 25,000 in case of permanent total disablement from injuries other than loss of limbs or death. The financial assistance is extended to the tune of Rs. 10,000 to the nominee of the deceased worker in case of natural death and Rs. 2,000 to meet the funeral expenses. Assistance of Rs. 1,000 for the education of the son or daughters of the workers passing 10th Standard examination, Rs. 1500 for passing plus two examinations and studying in regular bachelor degree course and Rs. 2,000 in case of post graduate course or professional course for every academic year is provided through the fund. A sum of Rs. 2,000 is extended to the applicant or his son or daughter for marriage. Further, assistance is also extended for delivery or the miscarriage or pregnancy or the termination of pregnancy by a registered female worker to the extent of Rs. 2,000.

In addition to governmental efforts, several public institutions and agencies are also providing various kinds of social security benefits to selected groups of workers. Two of the outstanding examples are those of Self-Employed Women's Association (SEWA) and the Mathadi Workers Boards in Maharashtra. The social security experiments of SEWA started in 1975 with a demand from members for a maternal protection scheme followed by health care and childcare. This was followed by starting of an insurance programme in collaboration with insurance companies. The insurance scheme started by the SEWA Bank was based on a realistic estimate of the capacity of the members to pay the premium. An Integrated Insurance Scheme introduced by SEWA for its members, offers several benefits for a consolidated annual premium of Rs. 45. While SEWA itself provides some of the benefits, it works as a nodal agency to get cover under various policies separately for specific benefits from different insurance companies. The risk covered includes health costs up to Rs. 1,000, maternity benefit of Rs. 300 and payment of varying amounts up to Rs. 10,000 in case of natural or accidental death including disablement of the member or her husband. The insurance scheme has turned out to be both popular and financially viable. The total coverage of SEWA social security scheme is about 50,000 women. The experience of SEWA reveals that in order to become effective, the social security scheme for the informal sector should be locally managed and controlled. Further, only such schemes will become viable which is need based and integrated with the economic activities of the local people. If poor people are supported through capacity building and necessary linkages are provided with their own economic activities the chances of success of social security efforts increased significantly. Further, it has demonstrated that, it is not only necessary to search new social security programmes but new social security organizations to run them.

A mathadi is a worker who carries a load on his head, back, neck or shoulders. Normally his work consists of loading, unloading, carrying, shifting, weighing, tapping, banding and stacking goods. In the State of Maharashtra, the Mathadi Labour Market is regulated by Mathadi Tripartite Boards set up since 1969. There are about 50,000 registered employers and 1,50,000 workers registered under 30 different boards in the State. The Mathadi Workers Boards, besides settling disputes between unions and employers, are actively involved in imparting social security benefits to their members by setting up of hospitals and dispensaries. At present there are two hospitals with an annual budget of Rs. 2 crores which are run by six Mathadi Boards. In addition to this, there are 12 dispensaries. Each of the six Boards contributes 2 per cent of their levy and each worker contributes Rs. 20 per month. These hospitals provide diagnostic services such as radiology, pathology and sonography for around 40,000 workers and their families. During the last few years, some of the Mathadi Boards have been able to get the workers registered with them insured against accident, injuries and death. For example, Mathadi

Boards in Pune are paying Rs. 152 per annum as premium out of the Board's administrative account to cover workers for a benefit of Rs. 25,000 in case of injury and Rs. 2,00,000 in case of death to each worker. This scheme has been worked out by the Mathadi Board with the General Insurance Corporation. Besides organizations like Co-operative Development Foundation (CDF), Trivandrum District Fishermen Federation (TDFF), the Association of Sarwa Sewa Farms (ASSF), the Society for Promotion of Area Resources Centre (SPARC), Voluntary Health Services (VHS) in Tamil Nadu and the Working Women's Forum have experimented for providing social security to small groups of people. The VHS in Chennai and the Association for Health Welfare in Nilgiris (ASHWINI) in the tribal areas of Gudalur in Tamil Nadu have made efforts to provide medical care to very specific target groups. The approach of these agencies is based on collecting of contribution from the beneficiaries themselves for their future contingencies in line with the insurance principles.

CONCLUDING REMARKS

In the developing economies a substantial share of employment is indeed in informal category and women in all age groups depend on the informal sector more heavily than men. Women are over represented in this sector in the sense that their share in the sector is higher than their share in total labour force. Most women tend to be own account workers and only a few are heads of micro enterprises. Relatively lower level of education among women, compared to men, seems to explain, in part, this gender differential in informal employment. Discrimination in the labour market also explains in part the disproportionate concentration as it limits women's access to formal and wage employment. Women also face additional constraints because of their homemaking and childcare responsibilities, which limits their participation in formal employment.

The concept of social security has been changing with the passage of time from traditional ways to modern forms of protection. While the definition of social security has been made comprehensive, however little attention has been paid to the working poor in the informal sector. The protection that a society provides to individuals and households to ensure access to wage and working conditions in a comprehensive sense, in matters of security of employment, health care, maternity benefits, provident fund, retirement benefits, is an essential element of the safety nets that keeps working people and their families from falling into poverty. Efforts to extend social security coverage to the informal sector face a number of challenges namely, inadequate social security expenditure as well as inefficient utilization of funds under government and non-government programmes; higher transaction costs due to the additional costs arising out enforcing compliance to extend social security coverage to the informal sector in urban and rural areas; non-existence of loan facilities and sponsorship for training to the workers in informal sector in the conventional social security protection schemes; lack of contribution capability due to low income to the existing insurance schemes for their future protection; lack of support from the workers to some non-statutory welfare funds having negligible benefits etc.

REFERENCES

Dasgupta, S. (2003), Women Organizing for Socio-Economic Security, *The Indian Journal of Labour Economics*, 46 (1): 39-68.

Djankov, S., Lieberman, I., Mukherjee, J. and Nenova, T. (2003), Going Informal: Benefits and Costs, In: Boyan Belev (ed.), *The Informal Economy in the EU Accession Countries: Size, Scope, Trends and Challenges to the Process of EU Enlargement*, Center for the Study of Democracy, Sofia.

Guhan,S. (1993), Social Security for the Poor in the Unorganized Sector: A Feasible Blueprint for India, In: K.S. Parikh et al. (eds.), *Human Development and Structural Adjustment*, Macmillan, Madras.

Hart, K. (1970), Small-Scale Entrepreneurs in Ghana and Development Planning, *The Journal of Development Studies*, 6 (4): 104-120.

International Labour Organization (1972), *Employment, Income and Equity: A Strategy for Increasing Productive Employment in Kenya*, Geneva.

International Labour Organization (2002), *Women and Men in the Informal Economy: A Statistical Picture*, Employment Sector Paper, Geneva.

Mahendra Dev, S. (2000), *Growth-Mediated and Support-Led Social Security in the Unorganized Sector in India*, Invest India Economic Foundation.

Rajan,I., Mishra,U.S. and Sarma, P.S. (1999), *India's Elderly: Burden or Challenge*, Sage Publications, New Delhi.

Sarkar, S. (2004), Extending Social Security Coverage to the Informal Sector in India, *Social Change*, 34 (4): 122-130.

Sarkar, S. (2006a), *Theorising Informal Economy*, Abhijeet Publications, Delhi.

Sarkar, S. (2006b), *Women Struggle for Sustainability*, Serials Publications, New Delhi.

Sethuraman, S.V. (1998), *Gender, Informality and Poverty: A Global Review*, World Bank, Washington, DC.

Subrahmanya, R.K.A. (2000), Support for the Unorganized Sector: Existing Social Security Measures, In: R. Jhabvala et al. (eds.), *The Unorganized Sector: Work Security and Social Protection*, Sage Publications, New Delhi.

Thomas, J.J. (1995), *Surviving in the City: The Urban Informal Sector in Latin America*, CT: Pluto Press, East Haven.

Chapter - 6

Gender and Shadow Economy

INTRODUCTION

The shadow economy represents all economic activity, which is not subject to direct taxation. It arises exclusively from government intervention, i.e. regulation and taxation. Such a policy intervention has side effects. Many empirical studies show that the size of the shadow economy has been most spectacular in the planned socialistic economies with maximum governmental intervention. However, Giles (1999) suggests that the size of the shadow economy has been growing over the past two or three decades in almost all of the countries for which comparative data have been assembled. According to Giles, growth in the underground economy is associated with increases in the actual or perceived tax burden but also with the degree of economic regulation. The view is shared by Thomas (1999) who describes that a growing shadow economy may be an indication of over-taxation and over-regulation. He also suggests that at least some part of the shadow economy may be social security fraud, making unemployment less bad as it looks. Schneider (2000) gives a concerned note by suggesting that under a growing or substantial shadow economy, policy is based on mistaken official indicators. In addition, he suggests that a growing shadow economy attracts workers to work in shadow economy and to work less in the official economy. Giles and Caragata (1999) are concerned that unpaid tax in hidden economy or loopholes allowing abusive avoidance in the existing tax system create a deadweight loss on the economy. These will, in turn, undermine taxation equity by shifting tax burden in the direction of honest, socially responsible individuals and corporations. Accordingly, part of the hidden economy is learned response to changing opportunities and constraints in fiscal policy, but on the other hand, there is a threshold level of underground activity that will sustain.

Theoretical attempts to analyze the shadow economy include Cowell (1989) who asks how far should taxation authorities go in pursuit of the missing income. Johnson et al. (1997) propose that supply of public goods tends to result in increasing returns in private firms, leading to multiple equilibria. Data on transition economies suggests that market-supporting institutions are critical for a successful transition. Friedman *et al.* (2000) suggest that the incentive to go underground to dodge higher tax rates is outweighed by the benefits of remaining official. Dabla-Norris and Feltenstein (2003) apply an inter-temporal general equilibrium model to explore the link between tax rates, access to credit and the size of the underground economy. Simulation results for Pakistan demonstrate that entry into underground economy can have a cyclical nature. Moreover, the share of underground activity will decline over time and sectors gradually move back into legal economy. With low taxes, there is no underground economy, but due to high budget and trade deficit the low tax regime is not sustainable over time. Thus an economy may have to accept some underground activity as part of an otherwise acceptable tax program. Research on the shadow economy focuses on the aspects of driving force in dealing with illicit work is the fact that these illegal and semi-legal activities are undesirable to official institutions. A growing shadow economy can be seen as the reaction of individuals who feel overburdened by the state and who choose the exit option rather than the voice option. If the increase of the shadow economy is caused by a rise in the overall tax and social security burden together with institutional sclerosis, then the consecutive flight into the underground may erode the tax and social security bases. The result can be a vicious circle of additional increase of budget deficit or tax rates, further growth of the shadow economy and gradual weakening of the economic and social fundament of collective arrangements. In addition, the effects of the shadow economy on the official one should also be taken into consideration because illicit work can be a source of allocation distortions, since resources and production factors are not used in the most efficient way. On the one hand, a growing shadow economy may attract workers away from the official labour market and create competition for official firms. On the other hand, at least two-thirds of the income earned in the shadow economy is spent in the official economy, thereby having a positive and stimulating effect on the official economy. Furthermore, a prospering shadow economy may cause severe difficulties for politicians because official indicators, e.g. on unemployment, labour force, income, GDP and consumption, are distorted. Policy based on erroneous indicators is likely to be ineffective, or even worse. Therefore, the reciprocal effects between the shadow and the official economy have to be considered when planning measures of economic policy, especially fiscal policy. The shadow economy is foremost a challenge both for economic theory and economic policy as answers have to be found to questions, such as why people work illicitly, why transactions are made in the shadow economy and what are the effects resulting from this behaviour. Currently, there are theoretical approaches in different social sciences, which concentrate on individual aspects of this complex phenomenon. As a coherent, integrative and interdisciplinary approach for the analysis of the causes is missing, however, it is necessary to develop a basic systematic model. Empirical studies have to test the methods for measuring the size and conceptualizing the development of the shadow economy, the theoretically derived causes and consequences of shadow-economic activities have to be verified; reverse effects on the official economy as well as the interaction between the two sectors have to be analyzed. The most difficult task for economic policy analysts is to convey the often not very much appreciated results of their work to politicians and to convince them that the findings are correct and relevant. But our suggestions with regard to specific economic policies are based on an analysis of the relationship between the causes and the effects of the shadow economy.

EXISTING LITERATURE

The general view in the literature is that the shadow economy is a manifestation of some kind of crisis (Weiss 1987) that is of the malfunctioning of an economic system. Excessive taxes, increases in social security contribution burdens and regulations are generally held responsible for the existence as well as for the growing size of the shadow economy. Unemployed are assumed to have an even higher incentive to work in the shadow economy due to their reduced income, plenty of leisure time, and clear disincentives to report their part-time work to the authorities because of an implicit marginal tax rate of nearly cent per cent. Another factor receiving more and more attention in the shadow economy literature are moral considerations, e.g. civic attitudes, tax morals etc.

Analyzing the literature on the underground economy, it quickly becomes apparent that the principal focus has been upon estimating its magnitude and how this varies either spatially or socially (Feige 1999). Taking as the starting point the marginality thesis that views underground work to be concentrated amongst marginalized groups and areas most studies have done little more than attempt to either corroborate or falsify this thesis (Williams and Windebank 1998). Although the steadfast popular belief in most western economies is that underground work is concentrated in marginalized populations, namely in deprived inner city localities (Blair and Endres 1994) and poorer peripheral regions (Button 1984), the vast majority of empirical studies show that this is not always the case and that it is frequently concentrated in affluent populations. Turning to why people engage in underground work, the predominant belief is that underground work is conducted under market-like work relations for profit-motivated purposes; it is a form of employment that people use and supply in order to make/ save money. Such a market-centered reading pertains both amongst those accepting the tenets of the marginality thesis which views such work to be conducted by marginalized populations (Blair and Endres 1994; Button 1984; Portes 1994) and those who recognize that it is more concentrated in affluent areas. This market-centered reading even predominates when multiple types of underground work are recognized ranging from its organized forms where such work is conducted for formal or informal businesses to its autonomous forms where it is undertaken on a self-employed basis. Consequently, even if underground work is no longer always viewed solely as an exploitative form of low-paid employment sitting at the bottom of a hierarchy of types of formal employment, but as a heterogeneous labour market with a hierarchy of its own, all such work remains widely viewed as market-like and profit-motivated, as displayed by the fact that this sector has been often discussed as a segmented informal labour market. More pertinently, such a market-centered reading also prevails when studies consider the geographical variations in the nature of underground work. This is the case whether underground work is seen to be composed mostly of exploitative organized forms of employment concentrated in deprived areas or a more refined approach is adopted that views residents in affluent areas as engaged in higher-quality underground work of the well-paid self-employed autonomous variety and the populations of deprived areas in lower-quality work of the poorer paid organized kind (Williams and Windebank 1998).

CAUSES AND CONSEQUENCES

There is a vast verbal literature on the possible determinants and consequences of the shadow economy. Obviously, as a sub-group of the shadow economy, the black economic activities are determined by almost the same determinants and have almost the same implications. In general, there are two major causes distinguished, as put forward by Gutmann (1977) and Tanzi (1980) namely, taxes and regulations. Gutmann (1977) argues that the government and its rules are the major reason for the existence of subterranean economy. According to Tanzi (1980), both of these factors can bring about an underground economy. Tanzi (1980) argues moreover that all kind of taxes causes some degree of underground activities. He also argues that if there were no taxes, there would still be underground economy because of various governmental restrictions on the activities of economic agents. The restrictions are imposed either because of inherently criminal or illegal reasons or for socioeconomic reasons. As these activities still use resources and generate incomes, they inevitably bring into existence the underground economy. Even some restrictions on legal activities cause the underground economy to some degree, in the form of underpayment of taxes or welfare payments, paying wages below the legal minimum etc. Frey *et al.* (1983) argue that factors such as tax morality, the vote of unemployment and the level development of an economy also be included as the consequences of the shadow economy. They argue that an individual feels that the government spends the taxes inadequately or as the unemployment level increases or economic development level is low, then there will be incentive for the individuals to participate in the shadow economy. Tanzi (1980) argues that the existence of a substantial underground economy would have important and, at times, disturbing implications for the measurement of macroeconomic variables, the pursuit of economic policy and the efficient functioning of the economy. For example, employment statistics may overestimate unemployment rates as a result of the underground economy. He also argued that the prices were likely to be lower in the shadow economy because of lower costs due to not paying taxes or not buying licenses to operate businesses; therefore the growth of the actual economy would be higher than the measured growth. Of course, as a result of these biased measurements in the crucial macroeconomic variables, the efficiency of monetary and fiscal policies will be adversely affected. The growth of the shadow economy has been caused by many different factors but the most important and most often cited ones are:

- The rise of the burden of taxes and social security contributions combined with the increase in the density and intensity of regulations in the official economy, especially on labour markets;
- The (forced) reduction of weekly working time, the early retirement and the growing unemployment rate, and
- The long-term decline of civic virtue and loyalty towards public institutions combined with a declining tax morale.

An interdisciplinary analysis of the causes of the increase of the shadow economy seems to be necessary as the economic factors can partly explain this increase. Micro-sociological and psychological approaches can provide very interesting additional insights in individuals' decision process choosing to work in the underground. In almost all studies, the rise of the tax and social security contribution burdens is one of the most important causes of the growth of the shadow-economy. Since taxes affect labour-leisure choices and stimulate labour supply in the shadow economy, or the untaxed sector of the economy, the distorting effect of this choice is a major concern of economists. The bigger the difference between the total cost of labour in the official economy and the after-tax earnings from work, the greater the incentive to avoid this difference and to work in the shadow economy. Since this difference depends largely on the social security system and the overall tax burden, they are key factors of the existence and the growth of the shadow economy.

A macroeconomic analysis of some of the causes for the increase of the shadow economic activities is given by Loayza (1996). He presents a simple macroeconomic endogenous growth model in which production technology depends on congestable public services. The determinants and effects of excessive taxes and regulations on the informal sector are studied; in the model the government lacks the capability to enforce compliance. The estimated coefficient of the independent variable, the direct tax burden (including social security payments), has the biggest influence, followed by the intensity of regulation and the complexity of the tax system.

The increase of the intensity of regulations, often measured by the number of laws and regulations, such as licenses requirements, is another important factor, which limits the freedom of choice for individuals engaged in the official economy. In this context one can think of labour market regulations, trade barriers and labour restrictions for foreigners. The influence of labour regulations on the shadow economy has also been analyzed in various studies. Regulations lead to a substantial increase in labour costs in the official economy. Since most of these costs can be shifted to the employees, these costs provide another incentive to work in the shadow economy, where it is possible to avoid them.

The numerous regulations on the official labour market and the total wage costs also represent driving forces for the shadow economy. Two main factors namely, the effects of the reduction in official working hours and the influence of the unemployment rate on the increase of the shadow economy.

The growth of the shadow economy leads to reduced state revenues, which, in turn, reduces the quality, and quantity of publicly provided goods and services. Ultimately, this can lead to an increase of the tax rates for firms and individuals in the official sector, quite often combined with a deterioration in the quality of the public goods (such as the public infrastructure) and of the administration, with the consequence of even stronger incentives to participate in the shadow economy. In a good number of countries the public sector is facing the challenge to impose substantial reforms of the social security and tax systems in order to prevent the total defeat of the protective welfare state, because the vicious circle of high tax and regulation burdens causes growth of the shadow economy, additional pressure on public finance resulting in higher tax rates, which, in turn, increase the incentives to evade taxes and to escape in the shadow economy and so on.

FACET AND TYPOLOGY

Research on the shadow economy focuses on three of its major aspects. In economic and social policy, the driving force in dealing with illicit work is the fact that these illegal and semi-legal activities are undesirable to official institutions. A growing shadow economy can be seen as the reaction of individuals who feel overburdened by the state and who choose the exit option rather than the voice option. If the increase of the shadow economy is caused by a rise in the overall tax and social security burden together with institutional sclerosis, then the consecutive flight into the underground may erode the tax and social security bases. The result can be a vicious circle of additional increase of budget deficit or tax rates, further growth of the shadow economy and gradual weakening of the economic and social fundament of collective arrangements.

In addition, the effects of the shadow economy on the official one should also be taken into consideration because illicit work can be a source of allocation distortions, since resources and production factors are not used in the most efficient way. On the one hand, a growing shadow economy may attract workers away from the official labour market and create competition for official firms. On the other hand, at least two-thirds of the income earned in the shadow economy is spent in the official economy, thereby having a positive and stimulating effect on the official economy. Furthermore, a prospering shadow economy may cause severe difficulties for politicians because official indicators, e.g. on unemployment, labour force, income, GDP and consumption are distorted. In social sciences, the shadow economy is foremost a challenge both for economic theory and economic policy as answers have to be found to questions, such as why people work illicitly, why transactions are made in the shadow economy and what are the effects resulting from this behaviour. Currently, there are theoretical approaches in different social sciences, which concentrate on individual aspects of this complex phenomenon. As a coherent, integrative and interdisciplinary approach for the analysis of the causes is missing, however, it is necessary to develop a basic systematic model. The most difficult task for economic policy analysts is to convey the often not very much appreciated results of their work to politicians and to convince them that the findings are correct and relevant.

Instead, reforms of the tax system and the social security system are necessary to improve the dynamics of the official economy and make the official institutions more competitive within the different institutional arrangements at national and international level. The discussion about adequate economic policies is often influenced by various ideological preferences. One can come across contradictory arguments ranging from a forced denial of the phenomenon shadow economy to imaginative exaggerations of its size and impact.

The starting point of nearly all controversies is the different estimates of the size of the shadow economy, which makes the assessment of the validity of the findings really hard. Due to this attitude, unfortunately, research efforts are fixated on questions, such as which is the best method to estimate the extent of the shadow economy, how large is the shadow economy labour force and how it changes over time. But the analysis of the causes and consequences of the increase of the shadow economic activities is much more important. Knowledge of these causes and effects on resource allocation, income distribution and stabilization policies as well as on the official economy in general provides the foundations for proposals for policy change on treating illicit work as an economic and social challenge.

Attention is drawn to the shadow economy due to the dramatically rising unemployment and the financing problems of public expenditure, as well as the rising vexation and disappointment with economic and social policies. Studies trying to measure the shadow economy first face the difficulty of defining it. For instance, one commonly used definition is the shadow economy includes all currently economic activities, which contribute to the officially calculated (or observed) GNP. However, Smith (1994) defines it as market-based production of goods and services, whether legal or illegal, that escapes detection in the official estimates of GDP. As these definitions leave open a lot of questions, Table 1 may be helpful for developing a better feeling for what could be a reasonable consensus definition of the legal and illegal, underground or shadow economy.

From Table 1 it becomes clear that the shadow economy includes unreported income from the production of legal goods and services, either from monetary or barter transactions hence, all economic activities, which would generally be taxable, were they reported to the tax authorities. In general, a precise definition seems quite difficult, if not impossible, as the shadow economy develops all the time according to the principle of running water, it adjusts to changes in taxes, to sanctions from the tax authorities and to general moral attitudes, etc.

Table 1
Shadow Economic Activities

Types of Activity	*Monetary Transactions*		*Non-monetary Transactions*	
Illegal Activities	Trade in stolen goods, drug dealing and manufacturing, prostitution, gambling, smuggling and fraud		Barter: drug, stolen goods, smuggling etc. Produce or growing drugs for own use. Theft for own use.	
Legal Activity	*Tax Evasion*	*Tax Avoidance*	*Tax Evasion*	*Tax Avoidance*
	Unreported income from self employment wages, salaries and assets from unreported work related to legal services and goods	Employee discount, fringe benefits	Barter of legal services and goods	All do-it-yourself work and neighbour help

Source: Lippert and Walker [1997].

INFORMAL VS. SHADOW ECONOMY

The informal economy is vertically stratified. The concept has sufficient flexibility and content to provide a suitable framework of analysis for the non-formal sector. It is an imperative segment of the labour market in many developing and transition countries. Starting from complete neglect, then phenomenon of informal economic activity has grown to be a subject of study by many researchers, both governmental and non-governmental. The informal economy is a part of survival and household strategies; nevertheless its contribution to well-being remains inadequately understood and largely unnoticed by policy makers. The recent phenomenal intensification of the informal economy and the rising interaction and interdependence of the formal and informal economy lead to growing interest in studies of the informal economy among many researchers and policy makers. The term informal sector and informal economy are used interchangeably to specify that segment of the economy and labour market, which has absorbed significant numbers of job seekers and unemployed workers outside government regulations and formal systems of labour and social protection. Studying the existing literature on the informal economy rapidly makes it evident that there is no standardized conceptual framework wrapping the subject. An extensive range of terms is used for numerous definitions or less precise descriptions of the phenomenon. Sometimes the similar term is used for diverse concepts and sometimes several terms portray the same concept. Various methods of research have been used to attain information on different concepts of the informal economy. The choice of methodology often resolves which part of the informal economy can be covered. This delves into why institutions or researchers interested in a specific definition and a specific coverage of the informal economy tend to use related approach and methodology. The scholars of the informal sector are still grappling with developing a concrete theoretical framework for what is undoubtedly a multifarious subject. However a key achievement of existing work on the sector is the legitimizing of the informal sector as a theoretical concept that calls for further empirical consideration.

There is a widespread feeling that a substantial and increasing share of activities takes place outside the formal economy. This holds, in particular, for developing and transition but also for high-income economies. Such activities are unrecorded by the system of national income accounting, which has become the accepted standard in all countries of the world. The existence and increase of an underground economy gives rise to three major sets of concerns. The economic and social conditions of individuals, household and countries are evaluated in a biased way if one relies on the official statistics. Thus, the official number of unemployed persons may hide that an (unknown) share of them actually work and receive wage income. As a consequence, the macro economic policies are likely to be too expansionary and social policy too excessive. A second concern is the loss of tax revenue as underground activities escape taxation. A third concern interprets the underground economy as an indicator of an unhealthy state between citizens and government. The taxpayers are dissatisfied with what public services they get for their contributions and seek to restress the balance by evading to the underground economy. It is feared that such reaction makes government unable to finance the public goods necessary for an economy and society. In contrast, opponents of government welcome such a development.

The phenomenon is known, and has been discussed in the literature, under many different names such as informal, unofficial, irregular, parallel second underground, subterranean, hidden, invisible, unrecorded and shadow economy or moonlighting. In several languages the term most often used is black economy. No single definition exists but it depends on the purpose. The most precise and predominantly used definition seeks to relate the underground economy to officially measured national income. It comprises all presently not recorded productive (i.e. value-adding) activities, which should be in the national product (GNP). This definition allows to compare and to add the underground economy to GNP. This definition excludes two major activities namely, production that by convention is not part of GNP, in particular private household activities and tax evasion is not value adding but redistribution and is therefore not included as such in the above definition (e.g. when taxes on interest payments are evaded). However, in general, no taxes are paid on underground activities (such as moonlighting for house building), which are value-adding. Thus, underground activities and tax evasion are related but certainly not identical.

The underground economy should neither be identified with illegality. Some activities are perfectly legal but are not subject to taxes (e.g. because of their small size), and therefore escape measurement in official statistics. Other activities are legal as such, but taxes are evaded. Finally, on illegal activities (such as drug production and distribution) no taxes are paid. Broader definitions of the informal and shadow economy, depending on their purpose, include private household production and redistribution activities.

The major emphasis of economists has been to measure the size of the shadow economy relative to official GNP; its size compared to other countries and its development over time. Three general sets of measurement approaches may be distinguished.

An obvious way to analyze the shadow economy is to undertake surveys among (supposed) suppliers and demanders of such services. This method allows to gather a detailed picture of the structure of this sector. However, because a substantial part of these activities is illegal, the interviewees may not be prepared to disclose their involvement. Somewhat surprisingly, research has shown this is no serious problem. Typically, men are more involved than women, the young more than the old, people without work more than employed ones, and the most prominent sectors are construction and all kinds of services. In contrast, where substantial capital assets (which are visible) are needed, less underground activity is observed.

A second direct approach is based on auditing of tax returns undertaken by tax collection and social security administrations. A sample of tax payers is scrutinized in depth and under threats of sanctions for failing collaboration. This approach provides detailed information on the strongest evaders, in particular the self-employed who have better opportunities for concealment. Capital income lends also easier to evasion than labour income. Tax audits have proved unable to reveal all tax evasion, and are limited to taxable activities. As a large part of tax evasion is redistribution, that part is not relevant to the narrow definition of the underground economy. A disadvantage of the two direct methods (surveys and tax auditing) is that they lead only to point estimates. Moreover, it is unlikely that they capture all shadow activities, so they can be seen as providing lower bound estimates. They are unable (at least at present) to provide estimates of the development and growth of the shadow economy over a long period of time. They have, however at least one considerable advantage-they can provide detailed information about shadow economy activities and the structure and composition of those who work in the shadow economy.

The shadow economy is reflected in discrepancies showing in various markets. Persons working in the unofficial sector are able to spend more than their officially recorded income. The discrepancy between the two may be observed at the level of individual households as well as in the aggregate national accounts. This approach is questionable as this expenditure income discrepancy may either be due to measurement errors (which is indeed often the case) or to reasons unrelated with the underground economy (e.g. the use of credits or reductions in wealth). Another discrepancy may be observable in the labour market. A decline in official participation rates, or a low participation rate compared to other countries, may be an indication of unofficial work. But again, the discrepancy may be related to other factors. Moreover, this approach is unable to isolate those persons who are at the same time active in the official and the unofficial economy (which is often the case). A third discrepancy may be visible in the monetary market. The dominant approach starts from the assumption that underground transactions are paid in cash in order to make detection more unlikely. The size of the underground economy is reflected in the amount of cash used in a country beyond that used for official transactions. This approach is elegant and easily applicable because the amount of currency is well documented.

Add to the model approach focuses on the causes and effects of the underground economy. By constructing a model, it seeks to identify the unobserved sector in-between. Three sets of factors are taken to be the main motivators of whether to engage in the unofficial economy: incentives to exit the official economy are the burden of taxation and of social security contributions, as well as government regulations. The latter hinder or even prohibit activities in the official economy (e.g. because of a lack in work permit, especially for foreigners), which provides an incentive to undertake them unofficially. This holds, of course, also for illegal activities such as the production and distribution of drugs. An important reason to exit the official sector is the restrictions imposed on working time. Low work hours, long holidays, early retirement, and above all unemployment are important reasons for moonlighting. Disincentives to be active in the underground economy are the expected punishment of doing so. It is composed of the probability to be caught and the size of punishment. For persons outside the established society (for example for illegal immigrants), or being self-employed, expected punishment is lower than for other persons, and therefore a higher rate of participation in the underground sector is likely. Another disincentive to be active in the underground economy is the moral costs entailed. A good citizen has moral qualms to undertake a forbidden activity. These moral costs are closely related to tax morale, which motivates citizens to pay their dues to the state. The effects of the underground economy are reflected in the traces visible in the labour, money and product markets discussed above. A specific econometric technique called unobservable variables allows to estimate the size of the underground economy lying between the causes and effects. This approach is the most comprehensive and builds on a well-structured behavioral model but it requires a large amount of data. As these are often not available (in particular not for developing and transition economies) this approach is not generally applicable. The estimation technique moreover tends not to be statistically robust.

CONCLUDING REMARKS

The analysis of the effects of a growing shadow economy is quite difficult and comprehensive empirical evidence is not available. Most studies focus on the influence on allocation of resources and the loss of revenue for the state. But the impact on the official institutions, norms and rules is even more important. The shadow economy can be seen as an indicator of a serious deficit of legitimacy of the present social order and the existing rules of official economic activities. Failing economic policy was confirmed as the most important cause for the burly increase in shadow-economic activities. Not only the rising tax burden and regulation density are important factors for the migration into the hidden economy, but also the defensive labour-market policy directed at a re-distribution of working hours. In addition, the lack of clear and stable institutions in transition countries is a driving force of informal economic activities. The tax deficit and evasion of social security contributions is the main arguments, with which the state wishes to substantiate its fight against the shadow economy. In combination with a reduced tax moral and less loyalty to the government, the potential of these factors will be exploited increasingly, which leads to the causes of the phenomenon call for to be addressed scientifically.

REFERENCES

Blair, J.P. and Endres, C.R. (1994), Hidden Economic Development Assets, *Economic Development Quarterly*, 8(3): 286-291.

Button, K. (1984), Regional Variations in the Irregular Economy: A Study of Possible Trends, *Regional Studies*, 18: 385-292.

Cowell, F.A. (1989), Honesty is Sometimes a Best Policy, *European Economic Review*, 33: 605-617.

Dabla-Norris, E. and Feltenstein, A. (2003), *An Analysis of the Underground Economy and Its Macroeconomic Consequences*, IMF Working Paper, 23/03.

Feige, E.L. (1999), Underground Economies in Transition: Non-compliance and Institutional Change, In: E.L. Feige and K. Ott (eds.), *Underground Economies in Transition: Unrecorded Activity, Tax Evasion, Corruption and Organized Crime*, Ashgate, Aldershot.

Frey, S.B. and Weck, H. (1983), Estimating the Shadow Economy: A Naive Approach, *Oxford Economic Papers*, 41: 23-44.

Friedman, E. et al. (1999), *Dodging the Grabbing Hand: The Determinants of Unofficial Activity in 69 Countries*, Discussion Paper, World Bank, Washington, D.C.

Giles, D.E.A. (1999), Measuring the Hidden Economy: Implications for Econometric Modeling, *The Economic Journal*, 109: F370-F380.

Giles, D.E.A. and Caragara, P.J. (1999), *The Learning Path of the Hidden Economy*, Econometrics Working Papers 9904, Department of Economics, University of Victoria.

Gutmann, P.M. (1977), The Subterranean Economy, *Financial Analysts Journal*, 33: 26-28.

Johnson, S., and Kaufman, D., Shleifer A., Goldman, M.I., and Weitzman, M.L. (1997), The Unofficial Economy in Transition, *Brookings Papers on Economic Activity*, (2): 159-239.

Lippert, Owen and Michael Walker (eds.) (1997), *The Underground Economy: Global Evidences of its Size and Impact*, The Frazer Institute, Vancouver, BC.

Loayza, Norman V. (1996), The Economics of the Informal Sector: A Simple Model and Some Empirical Evidence from Latin America, *Carnegie-Rochester Conference Series on Public Policy*, 45: 129-162.

Portes, A. (1994), The Informal Economy and Its Paradoxes, In: N.J. Smelser and R. Swedberg (eds.), *The Handbook of Economic Sociology*, Princeton University Press, Princeton, NJ.

Schneider, F. (2000), *The Increase of the Size of the Shadow Economy*, CESIfo Working Paper 306.

Smith, P.M. (1997), Assessing the Size of the Underground Economy: The Statistics Canada Perspective, In: Lippert, Owen and Michael Walker (eds), *The Underground Economy: Global Evidences of Its Size and Impact*, Fraser Institute, Vancouver, B.C.

Tanzi, V. (1980), The Underground Economy in the United States: Estimates and Implications, *Banca Nazionale Del Iavaro Quarterly Review*, 33: 427-453.

Thomas, J. (1999), Quantifying the Black Economy: Measurement without Theory yet Again? *The Economic Journal*, 109: F381-F389.

Weiss, L. (1987), Explaining the Underground Economy, *British Journal of Sociology*, 38: 216-234.

Williams, C.C. and Windebank, J. (1998), *Informal Employment in the Advanced Economies: Implications for Work and Welfare*, Routledge, London.

Chapter - 7

Vulnerability and Hidden Activities

INTRODUCTION

The informal economy as interacting with different forms of formal order viz., the financial/economic order (formal economy), the social order (national and city politics) and the criminal justice system. In some areas there is no clear dividing streak between formal and informal. Work typically done in the catering and leisure sectors in bars, cafes etc. is casual work, lowly paid, sometimes with the employer paying taxes and obeying health and safety or employment regulations (formal economy), sometimes not (informal economy). Equally, the dividing line between the informal economy sometimes called the 'grey' economy and the shadow (criminal) economy is also often blurred. Street trading of counterfeit or stolen goods, prostitution and dealing in drugs overlap the line between informal work (part-time prostitution by housewives, supplying drugs to friends) and organized crime. These fuzzy lines contribute to the difficulty there has been in providing adequate definitions and boundaries to the informal and shadow economies and hence, the formal economy which works across economic, sociological and social order/criminal justice discourses.

Some factors affecting the emergence and prevalence of particular forms of the informal economy are predominant. One is the kinds of opportunities which the geographical and trade situation of that city has encouraged and so which are available to people. To take a simple example, seasonal casual work picking fruit and vegetables can only exist where there is such agriculture and for crops where mechanized picking is either difficult to develop or very expensive (for example, apples). Street robbery is not very profitable in villages or residential neighbourhoods where there are few strangers and little passing pedestrian traffic. Drugs trading routes lead from producers to distributors to consumers, like any other commodity. Another factor is whether particular opportunities have been taken over by particular groups, to which entry is difficult. So, for example, the opportunities or the techniques may have been monopolized within ethnic groups, within cultural groups or by certain families. For example, prostitution on the street may be open to any women though being economically successful at prostitution tends to require youth and either attractiveness or technique. However, prostitution tends to occur in certain areas in cities areas, which remain red light areas for many years. Having a 'patch' of pavement from which to operate in a city may sometimes be difficult to acquire. The regulars may not look kindly on newcomers or there may be more or less organized attempts to secure particular patches for particular women. Nonetheless, newcomers in cities of developed countries are usually able to start prostitution on. Yet another factor is the extent to which seizing the opportunity requires acquiring skills and techniques and how these may be acquired. For example, some credit and cheque card fraud requires equipment and limited skill although much of this equipment is more available than many will realize. Other forms of fraud may require nerve or bravado, but hardly technical expertise. Equally, if the opportunity results in non-legitimate property, the person will need to convert the property into cash or legitimately held property. This is the market for stolen goods. If it results in lots of illegitimately acquired cash, the authorities are increasingly looking out for people depositing suitcases of grubby notes-there is now a market for stolen cash as well, which requires more specialized knowledge. The lack of trust in the legal system and the possibility for people to have influence on it in a non-transparent way are major issues. It is very difficult to get precise information in this area but it is obvious that petty corruption of law enforcement officials is widespread in the poorer countries of South Asia.

CONCEPTUALIZATION

While the divergence between informal and shadow activities is the subtlest, it is also imperative to discriminate between other forms of non-measured, non-taxed, and/or non-regulated activities. Several scholars have argued that a distinction can be made between households, informal, underground and illegal activities (ILO 1993; Thomas 1992). In fact, as much of the research in developing countries has revealed there is a continuum, not only between informal and formal activities, but also between household, informal, underground and illegal activities. However, for policy, measurement and analytical purposes it is important to distinguish between them. Initiating with the household sector, the informal sector could be defined as the set of activities, enterprises, income or persons, which satisfy certain characteristics and which are by definition, not part of the household sector, and so on (Sarkar 2006a; 2006b).

Thus the concept of the informal sector has sufficient flexibility and content to provide a suitable framework of analysis for the non-formal sector. In developing countries the debate on the informal sector has been mainly conceptual while in developed countries; it has been methodological, focusing principally on measurement techniques. Moreover, whereas in developing countries there is disagreement over what constitutes the informal sector, but agreement over what to call it, in developed countries there is general agreement over what it is but absolutely no agreement over what to call it. Thus the term informal economy has been used to fundamentally describe income or production, which escapes taxation and/or gross domestic product estimates (Sarkar 2005).

The diversity in definitions of the informal sector is a result of the fact that different units of observation and different criteria of informality have been used. Four main units of observation namely, enterprises, activities, income and people can be identified. Similarly, three main criteria used to determine informality such as registration (mainly for tax and social security purposes), measurement in GDP statistics and regulation; mainly labour regulation could also be recognized. The informal sector has been defined by any combination of the above units and criteria. Thus, for instance, it has been defined as the set of all income that escapes measurement, all enterprises that escape registration, all activities that escape regulation, all income that escapes registration, all people whose work escapes registration, all enterprises that escape regulation, and so forth. Although these concepts are related, they do not necessarily define the same thing. For instance, the 'registration' and 'measurement' criteria are often assumed to delineate the same group of observations (Kaufmann and Kaliberda 1996). However, activities that escape taxation are not necessarily activities that escape measurement of GDP. Moreover, only productive activities are included in GDP, whereas certain activities such as illegally exporting capital or concealing income on capital gains, are considered tax evasion but are not productive activities and therefore are not considered to be unmeasured GDP. Similarly, household activities such as agricultural production for own-consumption should be included in GDP, and would therefore be included in measures of the underground economy based on the measurement criterion, but are not considered part of tax evasion. In the same way, using income or productive activities as units does not necessarily measure the same thing, as certain taxable income is generated by non-productive activities such as capital gains. None of these criteria or units of observation are preferable to the others per se. Different units and criteria may be used depending on the aim of the research. However, it is important to make a conceptual distinction between those unmeasured, and/or unregistered and/or unregulated activities (income, enterprises, or people) whose primary purpose is to meet basic needs, from those, which are deliberately concealed to avoid taxes or regulations. This is particularly important in transition countries where, despite the focus of both policy and academic research on tax evasion, money laundering and corruption, there is increasing evidence of the existence and growth of an informal sector in the 'developing country' sense, as people turn to small-scale income and employment generating activities to generate livelihoods in the absence of sufficiently remunerated formal employment and social security (Anderson 1998; Bernabè 2002). By distinguishing between these two concepts, it is possible to analyze the extent to which these 'informal' income-generating activities provide a social-safety net, and the extent to which they undermine government revenue. This information will be critical for public policy, as it will allow the benefits of an increase in government revenue to be weighed against the risk of an increase in poverty, which would result from an attempt to 'tax' or 'eradicate' some of these income-generating activities without providing any other form of social security. The call to distinguish between the informal and the underground/hidden/unofficial sector or economy is not new. Thomas (1992; 1995) suggests that informal enterprises can be distinguished from irregular ones in that the latter involve the production of legal goods and services, but are illegal in the production or distribution process (because they evade taxes, social security contributions, or infringe other regulations), while the former involve legal goods and services and are 'quasi-legal' in their production or distribution process. They are 'quasi-legal' in that they are undertaken 'not to evade taxes, since their earnings are unlikely to be large enough to attract the tax collector, but because the authorities do not formally encourage such activities' (Thomas 1995).

Similarly, the Organization for Economic Cooperation and Development (OECD), the System of National Accounts (SNA) and the International Labour Office (ILO) suggest that 'activities performed by production units of the informal sector are not necessarily performed with the deliberate intention of evading the payment of taxes or social security contributions, or infringing labour or other legislations or administrative provisions. Accordingly the concept of informal sector activities should be distinguished from the concept of activities of the hidden or underground economy' (ILO 1993; OECD 1997; SNA 1993). However, the argument given is for a distinction between informal economic activities, and underground economic activities, irrespective of the type of enterprise in which they take place, whereas the ILO and OECD distinguish between activities that take place in informal enterprises and underground activities. The European Bank for Reconstruction and Development (EBRD) also differentiates between 'informal work undertaken to maintain subsistence levels' and 'informal labour motivated by market incentives such as tax evasion or the business environment' (EBRD 2000). It suggests that informal work has played a crucial role in the provision of employment and earnings for many people during the transition period but that the driving forces have differed across regions, with the poorer countries motivated by the lack of formal opportunities and a need to survive while in the more advanced countries the motivation has been more market-related including tax evasion and avoidance of bureaucratic delays and impediments (EBRD 2000). Finally, it is important to note that the use of motive (or intent) to differentiate between activities is common practice in both law and economics. As Cowell (1990) points out, from a legal perspective the distinction between (illegal) evasion and (legal but questionable) avoidance relies on the judge's perception of the intentions underlying the taxpayer's actions.

Existing literature on the shadow economy distinguishes the divisions of the total economy activities in several forms such as official-unofficial, formal-informal, registered-unregistered, observed-unobserved, formal-shadow, formal-underground, formal-subterranean, official-parallel, unhidden-hidden, regular-irregular, etc. A very convenient and simple definition of the total economic activities put forward by Smith (1986) and also adopted by Fagan (1997) is illustrated in Table 1. According to Smith (1986), total economic activities comprise all production of goods and services whether sold in markets or not. The formal economy is that portion of total economic activity, which appears in official estimates of national income. It includes both recorded market activity and non-market activity such as public administration and various imputations (e.g. rent on owner-occupied housing. According to Smith (1986), the shadow economy comprises that part of the total economic activity, which is excluded from the official measurement process. Some items are excluded for conceptual reasons (e.g. home production and gardening). However, other components are not recorded because of the desire of participants to conceal their activities (e.g. crime or tax evasion). Smith (1986) defines this component of the shadow economy as the black economy. He also defines the black economic activities in a broader framework, that these activities include various components of individual or corporate incomes, which are not reported to the authorities in order to evade taxation. For example, working while claiming unemployment benefits prostitution, selling illegal drugs and different types of financial frauds. In Fagan (1997), these black economic activities are presented in a systematic order (Table 2).

Table 1
Shadow Economy, Formal Economy and Black Economy

Formal economy			*Shadow economy*			
Non-market economy		Market activity	Black economy		Non-market shadow economy	
Imputed items	Government spending	Goods and services included in official GDP	Tax evasion	Crime production	Household economy	Voluntary work
Measured GDP			Activities that should, in principle, be included in measured GDP, but are not because they are hidden		Activities excluded from GDP by convention	
Total economic activity						

Source: Fagan [1997].

Table 2
Typical Activities in the Shadow Economy

Household and individual	*Private companies*
Incomes not declared for tax (e.g. income from second jobs, moonlighting, tips and gratuities under-reported self-employment income etc.)	Off the books business (sales that are unrecorded to reduce sales and profits liability tax)
Undeclared incomes in kind	False accounting for National Insurance deductions
Working and claiming	Private expenditures (cars, entertainment) put down as company costs
Production of illegal goods and services (e.g. drugs, prostitution)	Inter company barter

Source: Fagan [1997].

Therefore, the term hidden economy refers to the output from all productive activities, enterprises, income or people, which are unmeasured in gross domestic product and/or untaxed and/or unregulated. Thus the hidden economy comprises a wide range of productive activities from housework to organized crime. These can be grouped into four main categories namely, the household sector, the informal sector, the underground sector and the illegal sector. Add to, the household sector as the set of household productive economic activities that produce goods and services for own consumption within the same household and which are unmeasured and/or untaxed and/or unregulated because they are outside the SNA production boundary. The household sector includes those activities that fall within the general production boundary but not within the SNA production boundary. Some scholars have argued for the inclusion of non-quantitatively significant household activities in the SNA, particularly in developing countries where they may contribute considerably to livelihoods. In developing and transition countries where social services are extremely limited and incomes are very low, household activities are an important source of income and employment for a significant share of the population.

The informal sector is defined as the set of productive economic activities, which fall within the SNA (1993) production boundary and are unmeasured untaxed and/or unregulated, not because of deliberate attempts to evade the payment of taxes or infringe labour or other legislation, but because they are undertaken to meet basic needs. The ILO (1993) and SNA (1993) also argue for the need to distinguish informal sector activities from underground activities on the basis that the former are not necessarily performed with the deliberate intention of avoiding the payment of taxes, social security contributions or complying with certain legal standards, while the latter are. The ILO (1993) defines the informal sector as the set of units engaged in the production of goods or services with the primary objective of generating employment and incomes to the persons concerned. Production units of the informal sector are defined as a subset of household unincorporated enterprises. Household enterprises are units engaged in the production of goods or services which are not constituted as separate legal entities independently of the households or household members that own them, and for which no complete set of accounts are available which would permit a clear distinction of the production activities of the enterprises from the other activities of their owners and the identification of any flows of income and capital between the enterprise and the owners. Indeed, since its conception the informal sector has been of interest in developing countries because it is an important source of income and employment for the poor. It is a survival strategy in countries where there is insufficient formal employment opportunities, where wages may be too low to cover the cost of living and where social safety nets such as unemployment or pension benefits are either lacking or also insufficient to cover the cost of living. As such, it should include all productive activities, which generate income and employment for the poor, and not just those that take place in household enterprises with certain characteristics.

The concepts of underground and illegal production as defined in the SNA (1993) consists of legal productive economic activities that are part of the production boundary and are unmeasured and/or untaxed and or unregulated because they are deliberately concealed from public authorities for the following kind of reasons to avoid the payment of income, value added or other taxes; to avoid the payment of social security contributions; to avoid having to meet certain legal standards such as minimum wages, maximum hours, safety or health standards, etc. to avoid complying with certain administrative procedures such as completing statistical questionnaires or other administrative forms. The illegal sector consists of productive activities that generate goods and services forbidden by law or that are unlawful when carried out by unauthorized producers. There are two types of illegal activities: those that produce goods and services whose sale, distribution or possession is forbidden by law, and activities which are usually legal, but become illegal when carried out by unauthorized producers (SNA 1993). Furthermore illegal activities are included in the SNA production boundary if the transactions involved are based on mutual consent.

Studying the literature on the hidden economy soon makes it evident that there is no uniform conceptual framework covering the subject. A wide variety of terms are used for numerous definitions or less accurate descriptions of the phenomenon. Terms and definitions do not always correspond. Sometimes the same term is used for different concepts and sometimes several terms describe the same concept. Various methods of research have been used to obtain information on different concepts of the hidden economy. The choice of methodology often determines which part of the hidden economy can be covered. This explains why institutions or researchers interested in a specific definition and a specific coverage of the hidden economy tend to use related methodology. Statistical bureaus which produce national accounts, for example, use discrepancy methods to deduce which part of published national income can be attributed to hidden activities. An interdisciplinary analysis of the causes of the increase of the shadow economy seems to be necessary as the economic factors can partly explain this increase. Micro-sociological and psychological approaches can provide very interesting additional insights in individuals' decision process choosing to work in the underground. In almost all studies, the rise of the tax and social security contribution burdens is one of the most important causes of the growth of the shadow-economy. Since taxes affect labour-leisure choices and stimulate labour supply in the shadow economy, or the untaxed sector of the economy, the distorting effect of this choice is a major concern of economists. The bigger the difference between the total cost of labour in the official economy and the after-tax earnings from work, the greater the incentive to avoid this difference and to work in the shadow economy. Since this difference depends largely on the social security system and the overall tax burden, they are key factors of the existence and the growth of the shadow economy.

Studies trying to measure the shadow economy first face the difficulty of defining it. For instance, one commonly used definition is the shadow economy includes all currently economic activities, which contribute to the officially calculated or observed GNP. However, Smith (1994) defines it as market-based production of goods and services, whether legal or illegal, that escapes detection in the official estimates of GDP. In general, a precise definition seems quite difficult, if not impossible, as the shadow economy develops all the time according to the 'principle of running water'–it adjusts to changes in taxes, to sanctions from the tax authorities and to general moral attitudes etc. (Mogensen *et al.* 1995).

According to the conceptual framework, the informal sector is represented in Table 3 by the sum of cells 2, 3 and 4 (i.e. the area with horizontal lines). The underground sector

Table 3
Comparing Conceptual Framework

Types of Enterprises or units			*Unmeasured economic activities*			
			Out of SNA production boundary	*In SNA production boundary*		
				Legal		*Illegal*
				Aim is to meet basic needs	*Deliberately concealed to avoid tax or regulation*	
Unincorporated	Household	Informal own-account enterprises or Enterprises of informal employers		2	5	8
		Other (e.g. house hold enterprises producing for own-consumption)	1	3	6	9
	Non-house hold e.g. government			4	7	10
Other i.e. corporations, quasi-corporations, non-profit institutions						

Notes: Cells shaded in black represent activities that, by definition, do not exist. Cells that are blank do exist, but are outside of the conceptual framework. In the conceptual framework, the household sector = (1); the informal sector = (2)+(3)+(4); the underground sector = (5) + (6) + (7) and the illegal sector = (8) + (9) + (10).

is the sum of cells 5,6,7, the illegal sector is the sum of cells 8,9,10, and the household sector is represented by cell 1 (e.g. cooking, cleaning, caring for the sick etc). Note that for OECD (1997) and Thomas (1992) the household sector would be represented by cells 1 and 3 (i.e. they include all activities aimed at producing goods and services for own-consumption, including those that are in the SNA production boundary, such as subsistence agriculture in many developing and transition countries). Definitions in developing countries can be illustrated by the ILO (1993) definition, which can broadly be represented in Table 4 by the sum of cells 2, 5, 6 (i.e. the area with vertical lines). In this case, the informal sector is the set of informal own-account enterprises and enterprises of informal employers. According to this definition, activities undertaken in the informal sector can theoretically be underground or illegal (cells 5 and 8). Definitions in developed countries can broadly be represented by the sum of cells 2 to10. This includes all activities that should be measured, taxed or regulated, because they fall within the SNA production boundary, but are not. Note that it may also include other activities such as the evasion of taxes on capital gains, which we cannot represent in our matrix because they are not productive economic activities. Since definitions in transition countries have been extremely varied, definitions used by studies that have focused on how people survive during transition, can be represented by any combination of cells 2 and 3. Those, which have focused on measuring untaxed or unmeasured GDP, have defined it as any combination of cells 2 to 10 plus some other nonproductive activities such as capital flight. Finally, those which have focused on the transformation of economy into the informal economy are even more difficult to represent in the above table as they have included all private sector activity, which could include cells 2,3,5,6,8,9 and those parts of cells 4,7 and 10 which are in the private sector plus other non-productive activities such as theft, bribery and capital flight. Finally, definitions in centrally planned countries are equally difficult to illustrate in the above table and could be represented by the same cells as those of the above group that adopted second economy definitions.

INFORMAL-SHADOW ECONOMY AND FORMAL-SOCIAL ORDERS LINKAGES

The informal economy poses considerable concerns and threats, which have been documented in some previous research. In relation to the fiscal order, informal activities do not contribute in tax. Should they be taxed (prostitution is currently one of the main problematic areas)? What form of taxation might be appropriate–a tax burden falling on workers (income tax or VAT), a tax burden falling upon those who supply premises for the activity (property taxes), or a tax burden falling upon the more organized and possibly more profitable forms of the activity (company taxes)? Each form of taxation will target different aspects of the informal economic activity and differentially advantage particular forms. It will have the effect of discouraging certain forms and, consequently, seeming to advantage other forms, with allied social effects. High property taxes on brothels, for example, may increase street prostitution, which has unfortunate consequent effects upon others using the streets, including other women and children. The overall tax burden on the different forms of the informal economy can be termed the fiscal order. The fiscal order tends to be set at a national level, with only minor variations between cities or regions. The fiscal order is not the same as the economic order. The economic order concerns the economic effects of the informal economy.

In several countries, certain economic sectors are to some degree reliant on the low wages and lack of regulation characteristic of the informal economy. The agricultural, catering and tourism sectors are the most obvious, with seasonal work being common in the agricultural sector and now resulting in relatively organized forms bringing in seasonal workers from other parts of the country or even other countries, used to lower wages. Catering is increasingly regulated on hygiene grounds, but bar staff are still often casual workers. The economic order is far more differentiated geographically than the fiscal order, with different regions and cities having varying dependence on tourism or agriculture. Therefore, fiscal preferences for taxing also immediately pose problems of whether so doing implies condoning the threats to the social order posed by the same activities, which may breach city-wide policies for control of their symptoms, designed to promote social order (zoning, environmental policies, health and safety, employment law). Not only is there a regulatory question about the balance to be struck between tolerance and control (as well as one about the often conflicting demands between different population groups - for example, in relation to prostitution, residents and curb crawlers), but also one about the criminal justice order and the extent of policing. The preventive approach adopted by regulators to the kinds of work places typical of the informal economy (trying to improve workers' conditions) comes up against the retributive approach of traditional policing (prosecute them for currently illegal activity) and the exclusionary approach of immigration regulation (deportation etc.). From a bottom-up perspective of those seeking employment, however, the informal economy provides opportunities, albeit accompanied by potential threats–the impossibility of complaining about conditions, illegal activities etc. It is important to explore the choices available in the employment market for different kinds of people in the city. These will be linked to the population groups, the raw materials available (tourists etc.), formal employment opportunities (minimum wage thresholds, etc.), general economic conditions and cultural factors. Though the criminal justice order is often a national one though there are often significant regional variations, social order is normally governed by citywide policies for regulation, planning, community safety and economic regeneration. Those most likely to work in the informal economy tend to come from poorer sectors of the community and their employment opportunity horizons are citywide, rather than national. Though informal social control operates at a much more localized level than cities (neighbourhoods, streets, clusters of houses, tenements), yet it is affected by citywide policing cultures. The framework for the exploratory work hence involved consideration of different forms of the informal economy, and their links with the formal and shadow economies. Both threats and opportunities needed to be taken into account, so that it is possible to consider both the control environment and employment structures. The field needs to be dominated by multi-disciplinary, comparative focus.

ESTIMATING, EXPLAINING AND COUNTERACTING

The essence of an informal economy is to escape from being measured and captured; therefore both definition and methodologies shall be treated only as a way of approximation more than elsewhere in the economy in general. The informal economy is particularly flexible in reacting to changes in the regulatory framework-every new prohibition or regulation widens its scope and size. The informal economy exists in all countries, although those, which are in a process on transition, provide additional space for its existence. From the perspectives of policy decision-making finding measures that would make informal business activity less attractive is crucial. For the shadow sector to contract and, more importantly, for the formal economy to expand, it is essential to have:

- Minimum taxes and regulations, including legal provisions on starting a business, employment regulations, licensing rules etc.;
- Simple and efficient administration;

- Equal and transparent rules (e.g., no tax exemptions, minimal discretionary powers of public officials to interpret and apply legal provisions) and small bureaucracy;
- Clear procedures for settling tax and other business disputes;
- Reasonable fines;
- Property and business security (e.g., law enforcement);
- Stability of the legal system;
- Corporate development (more companies investing in brand name, publicity, etc.);
- Adequate general level of income.

Table 4
Size of Shadow Economy

Country	*% of GNP at end of 1990s**
Developing Countries	
Africa	
Nigeria and Egypt	68-76
Tunisia and Morocco	39-45
Central and South America	
Guatemala, Mexico, Peru and Panama	40-60
Chile, Costa Rica, Venezuela, Brazil, Paraguay and Columbia	25-35
Asia	
Thailand	70
Philippines, Sri Lanka, Malaysia and South Korea	38-50
Hong Kong and Singapore	13
Transition Economies	
Central Europe	
Hungary and Bulgaria	24-28
Poland and Rumania	16-20
Slovakia and Czech Republic	7-11
Former Soviet Union Countries	
Georgia, Azerbaijan, Ukraine and Belarus	28-43
Russia, Lithuania, Latvia and Estonia	20-27

* Estimates based on the physical input demand approach.

Table 4 provides a rough comparison of the size of the shadow economy relative to official GNP for a selection of developing and transition economies for the end of the 1990s, using the physical input demand approach. Some of these countries (Nigeria, Egypt, Thailand) are estimated to have an underground sector nearly three quarters the size of officially re-corded GNP. In many countries the size is one quarter to one third of GNP. In Asian countries with a comparatively low public sector, high tax morale or high expected punishment (Hong Kong, Singapore) the underground economy is estimated to be similar to that in many northern European countries.

Table 5 reports estimates of the growth of the shadow economy relative to GNP for selected Western countries and the United States, using the currency demand approach. The Scandinavian (Sweden, Norway, Denmark) and the German speaking countries (Germany, Austria) exhibit a sizeable increase of the shadow economy within the 35 years (1960-1999) covered. But also the countries with a low share in the beginning (Switzerland, the United States) show a significant increase, for the U S the share more than doubled. Sizeable increases have been estimated, with few exceptions, for all types of countries and all kinds of approaches the increasing importance of the underground relative to the official economy are a robust phenomenon.

Table 5
Growth of Shadow Economy

Country	*% of GNP 1960**	*% of GNP 1999**	*Percentage Increase*
Sweden	2	18.5	16.5
Denmark	4.5	17.5	13.0
Norway	1.5	18.0	16.5
Germany	2	14.2	11.2
United States	3.5	9.5	6
Austria	0.5	9	6.5
Switzerland	1	6.7	5.7

* Estimates based on the currency demand approach.

CONCLUDING REMARKS

The informality could exacerbate poverty, either directly or indirectly, through increasing inequality in the access to services and opportunities, increased vulnerability, and human abuse. It is an important coping mechanism when formal systems have collapsed or are under immense stress. Informality comes at a cost–the inability to use government and some private sector services available to firms that fully comply with regulations. Many transition economies have experienced surging share of entrepreneurial activity in the informal sector. People recognize that informality is harmful to their standards of living and to the distribution of income in general, but in most cases they have no choice because there are no viable formal alternatives. In some cases, however, there is a perception that through informal means it may be possible to get better deals by playing on connections or just by appealing directly for the understanding of the service provider. Indeed, in countries where formal cost recovery for services has been imposed to try and reduce under-the-table payments, it is not clear that the poor have been made better off. Regardless of this, informal payments are very important as a coping mechanism for the poor. In the poorer South Asian countries informality as a coping mechanism is prevalent due to a number of very straightforward factors. The lack of fiscal capacity of governments, which has many consequences i.e., social benefits are too low to survive on; in some cases they are lower than the poverty line. Health and education are insufficiently provided and staff employed in the social services is underpaid, which stimulates informal payments. Second, the lack of capacity of state institutions, where capability to target benefits is low in part because of the large-scale informal sector but also because the capacity for outreach and support is limited. Consequently, it is very difficult for the state to target subsidies for the poor and to introduce users' fees for the wealthy. Moreover, nongovernmental organizations (NGOs) and civil society in the region are also weak and not sufficiently organized to carry out the sort of support and outreach. Third, the lack of formal organizations to support trade and economic activity i.e., private sector activities are limited while the poor are numerous. This is both a cause and a consequence of poverty. Regional imbalances have increased dramatically with the transition to a market economy, mostly because the substantial subsidies supporting poor and isolated regions were sharply reduced.

Add to, the shadow economy can be regarded as part of an evolutionary process, making economic and societal development increasingly dynamic. On the one hand, the societal pressure on deregulation and tax reduction is increased and, on the other hand, new innovative forms of living together and economizing outside the restrictions are fashioned which could be regarded as a test for the official sector. The growth of the shadow economy over the last decades and its effect on the official economy both in general perception and scholarly research has prevailingly been evaluated as a negative development which should be counteracted. It has also been noticed that many developing and transition economies would break down or function at a much lower level of production and welfare if the shadow economy did not exist. Estimates of the shadow economy can also be based on the discrepancy between income declared for tax purposes and that measured by selective checks. Fiscal auditing programs have been particularly effective in this regard. Designed to measure the amount of undeclared taxable income, they have been used to calculate the shadow economy in several countries.

REFERENCES

Anderson, J.H.(1998), *The Size, Origins, and Character of Mongolia's Informal Sector During Transition,* World Bank, Washington, DC.

Bernabè, S. (2002), *A Profile of the Labour Market in Georgia,* ILO/ UNDP.

Cowell, F.A. (1990), *Cheating the Government: The Economics of Evasion*, Massachusetts MIT Press, Cambridge.

EBRD(2000), *Transition Report,* European Bank for Reconstruction and Development, London.

Fagan, P.G. (1997), The Black Economy in Ireland, *Irish Banking Review,* Summer: 19-25.

ILO (1993), *Resolution Concerning Statistics of Employment in the Informal Sector,* Geneva.

Kaufmann, D. and Kaliberda, A.(1996), *An 'Unofficial' Analysis of Economies in Transition: An Empirical Framework and Lessons for Policy,* Harvard Institute for International Development, Cambridge.

Mogensen, G.V. *et al.* (1995), *The Shadow Economy in Denmark 1994: Measurement and Results,* Study No. 3, The Rockwell Foundation Research Unit, Copenhagen.

OECD (1997), *Framework for the Measurement of Unrecorded Economic Activities in Transition Economies,* OECD, Paris.

Sarkar, S. (2005), The Conceptual and Theoretical Framework of Informal Economy: A Review of Literature in Developed and Developing Countries, *Journal of Social and Economic Policy,* 2(2): 187-205.

Sarkar, S.(2006a), *Theorising Informal Economy,* Abhijeet Publications, Delhi.

Sarkar, S. (2006b), *Women Struggle for Sustainability,* Serials Publications, New Delhi.

Smith, S. (1986), *Britain's Shadow Economy*, Clarendon Press, Oxford.

Smith, P. (1994), Assessing the Size of the Underground Economy: The Canadian Statistical Perspectives, *Canadian Economic Observer,* Catalogue No. 11–010, 3.16–33 at 3.18.

System of National Accounts (SNA) (1993), *System of National Accounts 1993,* World Bank, Washington, D.C.

Thomas, J.J. (1992), *Informal Economic Activity*, Harvester Wheatsheaf, Hemel Hempstead.

Thomas, J.J.(1995), *Surviving in the City: The Urban Informal Sector in Latin America,* Pluto Press, East Haven: CT.

Chapter - 8

Energy Security for Poor

INTRODUCTION

The vulnerable women suffer from the larger level of bribes than the non-poor households. With the difficult economic conditions of transition, a number of women no longer value edification as much as they did before the transition; their pinnacle priority is mere survival. In most ethnicity, women and men have differing roles and responsibilities according to socially defined division of labour based on gender. This gender inequity is reflected in a variety of social and economic dimensions. In terms of reproductive activities, women generally have primary responsibility for the care and feeding of children and families, as well as health care and education. In many developing countries, it is the women who perform most of the work related to subsistence agriculture, plus gathering and managing fuel and water as a part of the household responsibility. Their productive activities are often unpaid and labour-intensive. When women in rural areas do generate income, it tends to be within the informal sector, and not adequately reflected in national accounting systems. This serves to under-represent the importance of energy as an input to women's economic activities. Because they operate mostly in the informal and unpaid sectors, poor women have less access to financial resources, credit and equipment than do men, and less of a voice in household, or community-level, decision making. Gender-poverty is a problem that has a disproportionate effect on women and girls, especially in rural areas. The most obvious factors relate to time and physical effort. Many women in developing countries have to spend long hours gathering fuel and hauling water, using their own labour to carry heavy loads over long distances in addition to other informal work. When women are overburdened, they are more likely to keep their daughters home from school to assist with own household activities, including fuel and water collection, thereby limiting opportunities for girls to move forward through education, and rising the likelihood that their families will remain in poverty.

The concentration of indoor air pollutants coming out from combustion of biofuels such as wood, agriculture crops and dung cake used by rural households in developing countries cause severe health problems especially to women and children below five years. Mothers and their children spend an average of six hours per day in highly polluted indoor areas It has been estimated that approximately half the global population and up to 90 per cent of rural households in developing countries still rely on biomass fuels and about 75 per cent of Indian households use biofuels for cooking purposes (Sarkar 2005). Typically cooked indoors in open fires or poorly functioning stoves, which leads to levels of air pollution that are among the highest ever measured. Therefore indoor air pollution with biofuels is an issue that requires to be addressed through gender, energy, environment and health policy. Some of highest concentrations of pollutants come about due to the use of biofuels for cooking in rural indoor environment (Sarkar 2004a). In developed countries transformation has without exception been come with by a shift from biofuels to petroleum products (kerosene, LPG) and electricity. In developing countries even where cleaner more sophisticated fuels are available, households often continue to use biomass (Smith 1987). Although the portion of global energy derived from biofuel has fallen substantially which is evidence that biofuels use is increasing among the poor. Poverty is one of the main hurdles to the adoption of cleaner fuels and slow pace of development in many countries implies that biofuels will continue to be used by the poor for many years.

The informal economy is vertically stratified. The concept has sufficient flexibility and content to provide a suitable framework of analysis for the non-formal sector. It is an imperative segment of the labour market in many developing and transition countries. Starting from complete neglect, then phenomenon of informal economic activity has grown to be a subject of study by many researchers, both governmental and non-governmental. The informal economy is a part of survival and household strategies; nevertheless its contribution to well-being remains inadequately understood and largely unnoticed by policy makers. The recent phenomenal intensification of the informal economy and the rising interaction and interdependence of the formal and informal economy lead to growing interest in studies of the informal economy among many researchers and policy makers. The term informal sector and informal economy are used interchangeably to specify that segment of the economy and labour market, which has absorbed significant numbers of job seekers and unemployed workers outside government regulations and formal systems of labour and social protection. Studying the existing literature on the informal economy rapidly makes it evident that there is no standardized conceptual framework wrapping the subject. An extensive range of terms is used for numerous definitions or less precise descriptions of the phenomenon. Sometimes the similar term is used for diverse concepts and sometimes several terms portray the same concept. Various methods of research have been used to attain information on different concepts of the informal economy. The choice of methodology often resolves which part of the informal economy can be covered. This delves into why institutions or researchers interested in a specific definition and a specific coverage of the informal economy tend to use related approach and methodology. The scholars of the informal sector are still grappling with developing a concrete theoretical framework for what is undoubtedly a multifarious subject. However a key achievement of existing work on the sector is the legitimizing of the informal sector as a theoretical concept that calls for further empirical consideration in household energy sector.

In the developing economies a substantial share of employment is indeed in informal category and women in all age groups depend on the informal sector more heavily than men. In India the informal sector employs over 90 per cent of the workforce (Sarkar 2004b). Women are over represented in this sector in the sense that their share in the sector is higher than their share in total labour force. Most women tend to be own account workers and only a few are heads of micro enterprises. Relatively lower level of education among women, compared to men, seems to explain, in part, this gender differential in informal employment. Discrimination in the labour market also explains in part the disproportionate concentration as it limits women's access to formal and wage employment. Women also face additional constraints because of their homemaking and childcare responsibilities, which limits their participation in formal employment. Even within the informal sector more women than men seem to be in poor quality employment. In Latin America more women seem to be in the unpaid categories than men. In Africa the proportion of unpaid workers working in family owned enterprises among women appears to be relatively high compared to other regions. The causes for participation in the informal sector can be economic and non-economic. Economic reasons are related to unemployment and an inflexible formal labour market, a declining real price of capital and the high cost of formal production. Besides, non-economic causes are concerned with a greater flexibility and satisfaction in work, a complete use of workers professional qualifications and increased leisure time. There are two groups of factors, which determine the decision to become active in the informal sector, more specifically, the structural as well as opportunity factors. The structural factors consist of financial pressure, socio-psychological pressure and institutional constraints. The opportunity factors consist of individual background, skills, education, living condition or non-individual components, environment, values, standards etc. (Sarkar 2004c).

ENERGY-POVERTY TRADE OFF

While all forms of life require energy, the need for energy comes in a variety of different forms and can be satisfied in many ways. In very poor societies the main forms of energy are likely to be animate energy provided by draft animals and human labour. Even the poorest people will also use some inanimate energy such as wood fuel, crop residues and dung (biomass fuels) mainly for cooking. These energy sources are often referred to as traditional energy sources to distinguish them from modern energy sources such as electricity, coal, oil and LPG. The essential features of modern energy sources are that they are in some senses more convenient (more energy per unit volume, are easier to store or distribute, or are more efficient at doing useful work). Clearly all-modern fuels and some traditional fuels are traded (wood fuel is increasingly traded for money, and charcoal is almost always traded) and are therefore known as commercial fuels to distinguish them from non-commercial fuels. While non-commercial fuels are not traded for cash, they are not free. This is because non-commercial fuels usually require considerable expenditure of time for their collection and processing and this time can have a high opportunity cost in terms of other things that the collectors usually women and children could be doing, including going to school, if they were not collecting fuel. In addition both non-commercial and commercial fuels may incur costs often called externalities on society that is not necessarily reflected in their price such as environmental damage. Some forms of energy from traditional biomass can be converted into more useful forms and are then known as modern biomass fuels.

It can be seen why people have a very strong desire to switch from kerosene to electricity for lighting. The implications of this reality for poverty are as under.

- The energy use per unit of output can be higher in subsistence agriculture than in modern agriculture because the energy used in subsistence is largely animate and the conversion efficiency is very low.
- Agricultural output by poor people can be very much higher per unit of commercial energy input than modern agriculture. This is not necessarily good for development, but results from the fact that poor people often use very little or no commercial energy.
- Conventional modern forms of energy (fossil fuels, and electricity) will remain the fuel of first choice for many poor people for many years to come, while biomass fuels will remain the main fuel of necessity.
- Biofuels in the form of wood, crop residues, brush and animal dung is today still the chief form of inanimate energy for the majority of humanity, just as it has been since the discovery of fire.
- Energy statistics can be misleading as they are usually confined to commercial energy. However approximately one third of all energy consumption in developing countries derives from the burning of wood, crop residues and animal dung, and by some estimates it amounts to 1,000 million tons of oil equivalent per year, or more than three times the coal mines in Europe in a single year,

and twice the energy of the coal mines in the US and China (World Bank 1996).

- People in developing countries rarely cook with electricity.
- It is clearly misguided to suggest that developing countries have abundant free sunlight (or wind or falling water) and that this will solve their energy needs. While having these resources is probably better than not having them, the cost of making energy useful for specific applications (such generating electricity) is often very expensive.

One possible reason for the neglect of energy in recent development policy is the considerable growth in attention directed to the environmental consequences of obtaining, converting and using energy. These impacts include:

- Greenhouse gases from the burning of fossil fuels.
- Acid rain from burning of fossil fuels.
- Particulates, and the chemicals that cause smog in urban air as a result of fuels used in transport and industry.
- Deforestation and damaging the ecosystem from the collection and use of biomass fuels.
- Oil spills.
- Smoke from burning of forests, oil and gas field fires, and fires in coal mines.

There is no longer much doubt that global warming is likely to exacerbate the problems of those parts of the world that are already deeply stressed, economically and environmentally. It is also clear that if the poorer countries of the world were to consume per capita as much energy as industrialized countries currently do, global warming would be severe and probably irreversible. But the fact remains that under current prices and other incentives actions to reduce energy poverty can harm the environment, and vice versa. There is therefore a strong trade-off between the objective of tackling energy poverty and the objective of improving the environmental problems linked to energy conversion and use.

In the majority of cases the energy options that deal best with poverty will involve fossil fuels, and they can have a negative effect on the global environment. There are very few alternatives to fossil fuels for transport (although, Bangladesh still has a huge commercial in-land sailing fleet), the cheapest electricity for many people will come from large power stations fuelled by gas, coal, or even oil. Even in remote rural areas, diesel engines will provide the best solution for providing both shaft power and electrical energy.

A key dimension of the trade off between energy poverty and the global environment is that the benefits and burdens of the choices involved fall on different social groups, and that they occur in different parts of the world. The trade-off is therefore fundamentally a problem of political economy. It is currently the richer social groups in the world that are contributing most to global pollution, while it is the energy poor who are the ones being asked to restrict their choice to renewable energy options. People who currently do not have access to modern forms of energy cannot be expected to restrict their energy options just for renewable sources. They must be empowered to make informed choices between the full menus of energy options, so that they can select the option that best meets their needs. They certainly cannot be expected to restrict their options willingly, while northern industrialised countries are not doing enough to reduce the pollution burden of their current and past energy consumption.

ENGENDERING ENERGY

While it may be accepted that energy is an important input to development, it is conceptually and empirically difficult to attribute measurable poverty impacts to relatively small investments, such those associated with improving access to modern energy services. This is because in such cases there are many other circumstances, such as climatic variation and macro economic change, which affect the measurable poverty status of remote communities over any particular time period. Similar problems arise in trying to prove the causal links between any small development project and reduction in poverty, and between inputs, such as improved water supply, and improved health status. However it can be asserted that there is strong reason to believe that such inputs are likely to produce positive benefits. Most current impact evaluation work attempts to track the increased use of energy of poor people before and after the intervention rather than the impact on poverty itself. The importance of all this for poverty is that the choice of end-use is therefore not only crucial to the financial viability of decentralized energy investments, but they are crucial to the extent and distribution of those benefits.

In addressing energy poverty it is crucial to understand and deal with the gender dimension. It is well known that women and children usually form the majority of the poor people in any community. But what is probably less well known is that women are usually major users and suppliers of energy resources in marginalized communities. Women collect much of the biomass used by households, and women manage most of the energy used by households. Furthermore, as suggested earlier women also suffer the main health costs of using biomass fuels in inefficient stoves in a confined space. If energy services are provided to tasks that are traditionally considered in the woman's domain in many societies this will include agro processing, textiles, pottery, soap making etc. or are new activities not yet dominated by men, it can have a considerable (targeted) impact on women's lives.

The urban poor may have even greater problems with fuel scarcity as their incomes have not kept pace with the rising prices and they cannot fall back on subsistence production or their own labour in fuel gathering. A recent survey in Addis Ababa found that over two-thirds of the cash income of the lowest income group is spent on cooking fuel. Many of the fuel-saving strategies adopted by this group are deleterious to nutrition and health. Because they cannot afford the kind of stoves needed to burn more efficient fuels, the poor continue to rely on wood fuels even though their cost is as high as or higher than kerosene, gas or electricity. Official subsidies often favour modern fuels, overlooking the inability of the poor to either switch to a modern fuel or support the costs of traditional fuels. Measures are therefore urgently needed to enable poor urban households to meet their minimum basic energy needs. In villages where women have to spend more time on fuel collection, they compensate by spending less time on cooking, which can result in lower nutritional levels. Spending less time on cooking is an extreme reaction to fuel shortage. Cooking fewer meals, eating cold or leftover foods, snacks or processed foods and even changing diet have been reported as fuel-saving strategies in the Sahel countries, Haiti, Mexico and Nepal. Additionally, many of women's key income generating activities such as food processing, beer brewing, and fish smoking are fuel-intensive and difficulties in procuring adequate supplies of fuel threaten this income. The quantities and types of foods cooked play an important role in determining fuel use per head. Coastal villages in Peru and Ghana where fish consumption is high use much less cooking fuel than inland villages relying on hard staples such as maize, cereals, potatoes and cassava. This suggests that studies on fuel-saving methods should look carefully at foods requiring high energy inputs. This research indicates that between 5 and 20 per cent of household expenditure goes on fuel mainly kerosene and between 50 and 91 per cent on the food budget. Due to low cash incomes, even this minor use of commercial fuel affects food and other expenditure. This trend will continue unless rural incomes rise. Water boiling and heating were found to be luxury uses of fuel and are frequently curtailed when fuel is scarce. However, washing is essential for health and heating is often essential for survival. In cold mountainous regions such as the Andes, Himalayas and Ethiopian highlands, as much fuel may be used for heating as for cooking. Indoor air pollution is a further health problem in biomass-dependent areas.

The heavy overall workload imposed on women, including carrying fuel wood, affects their health, particularly if their energy output exceeds their intake. Fuel loads weighing 25-35 kg on average, and often much more, are carried over long distances. And while forest workers are provided with special equipment for their work, women who collect fuel for subsistence must do so with their bare hands and primitive tools. Women are hardest hit by this crisis since they are largely responsible for subsistence food production and must increase their labour inputs when productivity decreases. Moreover, male assistance for land clearing and ploughing is often no longer available due to migration an avenue often closed to women for social mobility reasons. Similarly, as the quality and quantity of forest and water resources decline, the time and effort that must be devoted to fuel and water collection, two of women's traditional tasks, also increase. Women therefore have to work harder and longer, using child labour to help them. They are forced to cut down on family living standards, while at the same time they try to squeeze more output and income from the land thereby often contributing to the destruction of the ecological base. These are among the major findings of an ILO research project on energy and rural women's work in several Asian, African and Latin American countries, carried out by multidisciplinary national teams. The studies showed that, confronted with changes in fuel availability due to deforestation, rural households are being forced to make various adjustments that adversely affect their living standards. The adjustments produce negative effects on work patterns, family nutrition and health, the environment, agricultural productivity, and incomes. These in turn have a bearing on the urban fuel crisis. The double and triple burden on rural women of household maintenance, family agricultural tasks and income generation, means that in the countries studied, women work considerably longer hours (11-14 hours daily) than men (8-10 hours daily). In virtually all the villages observed, cooking and fuel collection were two of the most time-consuming activities (Cecelski 1987).Therefore women's work is closely linked with the land in terms of water, fuel and fodder collection, and processing of food crops. The increase in cultivated land and the corresponding loss of grazing land has resulted in a decrease in the number of animals supported in the villages, and a correspondingly smaller amount of dung. Of this, proportionately more must be used as fuel due to shortage of wood. This has the effect of increasing women's work, as does the practice of stall-feeding animals rather than grazing them, which requires the investment of more time in fetching fodder and water.

CONCLUDING REMARKS

Unlike modern fuels, the supply of biofuels such as wood and charcoal are still largely uncontrolled and based in the informal sector. The supply of biomass fuel for the cities is also uncontrolled and in most cases, biomass production is unsustainable. Wood is felled in state-owned forests by dealers, but the cost of replacing the trees is not paid, with the result that forests are deteriorating rapidly around major cities. Past efforts to relieve the resulting firewood shortage by encouraging farmers to grow trees have largely failed because the costs of this far exceed the short-term costs of gathering fuel from existing forests. However new efforts to empower local communities to manage the forests in their areas in a sustainable way for the production, among other things, of biomass fuels are encouraging, particularly as this could provide income sources for the poor within the community. In most developing countries the majority of informal sector enterprises are owned and operated by women, with women making up the largest proportion of the work force. Despite this, the contribution of women entrepreneurs to national economies is not explicit in national statistics, leading to the development of policies that do not deal with the specific barriers faced by women linked to their gender-defined roles. Their enterprises tend to be concentrated in a relatively narrow range of activities such as knitting, dressmaking, crocheting, cane work and retail trading. These activities tend to have disproportionately low rates of return compared to the activities undertaken by men. However despite the low financial returns, women's enterprises provide important sources of household income, even in male-headed households. Women headed enterprises are frequently located in the home and these cottage industries tend to be overlooked by agencies because they are in the informal sector, which is diffuse and difficult to reach. When women are forced to close their enterprises, it is often for non-business reasons and linked to factors associated with working from home. The low rates of return prevent inward investment, hindering innovation and expansion, which are regarded as key factors in enterprise sustainability. There is little research to explain what forces drive these startups and shutdowns, and how gender influences these processes. Women's access to resources (such as credit, land and education, which are recognized as key factors in micro enterprise development) is significantly less than that of men. Generally, research in small and medium-scale enterprise sustainability indicates that a lack of working capital is one of the two most common causes of enterprise failure. Women's access to decision-making within the household and community is also restricted, reducing their ability to influence processes and resource allocation. Given the disproportionate number of poor women in rural areas, research which takes into account gender aspects of the transformation of structures and processes could make a significant contribution to the development of gender equitable sustainable livelihoods.

Policies for rural areas that encourage the uptake of efficient use of biomass fuels can effectively address the problem of indoor air pollution and physical drudgery of poor women. But women must involve in the planning of these policies and interventions to ensure their successful implementation and sustainability. Although the portion of global energy derived from biofuel has fallen substantially which is evidence that biofuel use is increasing among the poor in developing countries including India. Poverty is one of the main hurdles to the adoption of cleaner fuels and slow pace of development in many countries implies that biofuels will continue to be used by the poor for many years. Despite the magnitude of the problem of indoor air pollution, the health impact of this environmental exposure has been relatively neglected by researchers and policy makers. The foremost consideration for embarking upon development of sector specific interventions on gender, energy and poverty issues are to ensure sufficient institutional arrangements and subsequent strengthening of capacities. Thus establishment of a gender consultative group with representatives from government, private and civil society institutions would call for. This may be done by assigning a focal point within the group whose role would be vital in programme designing, implementation as well as monitoring and evaluation of gender and energy related programme. It is also important that sufficient technical support is available to this focal point for effective execution, which should come from the available international expertise within the civil society under the prerogative of the gender-environment consultative group.

While the State has certainly been rolled back from direct involvement in providing energy services to poor people in many developing countries, it still plays a crucial role both in providing subsidies but more importantly in creating a regulatory framework. Although the climate is growing more favourable to decentralized energy supply options, in most countries the existing regulatory framework is often the major barrier to development. It can be hostile, contradictory or uncertain. Taxes and subsidies often undermine markets, rather than encourage them. The supporting infrastructure of training institutions, or finance may be non existent or inaccessible. Competitors may be able to gain access to subsidies that enable them to sell their products below cost. Without changes to this policy environment, the flow of private sector finance and innovation will be restricted. These areas are currently the focus of analysis, innovation and reform.

The global environment, must not turn aside development policy and practice away from addressing the energy needs of poor people:

- Fossil fuels will remain the fuel of first choice for many poor people for many years to come, while biomass fuels will remain the main fuel of necessity.
- People who currently do not have access to modern forms of energy cannot be expected to restrict their energy options just to renewable sources, while northern industrialized countries are not doing enough to reduce the pollution burden of their current and past energy consumption.

In rural context, development and introduction of wood stores with chimneys and promotion of improved fire management techniques is needed to reduce smoke levels inside dwellings and improve the efficiency of fuel wood use. It is clear that opportunities exist for the improvement of the environment sustainibility of energy use in developing countries and local energy development priorities may contribute to the transformation of the section into a more environmentally and socially sustainable base for development.

REFERENCES

Cocelski, E. (1987), Energy and Rural Women's Work: Crisis, Response and Policy Alternatives, *International Labour Review*, 126(1): 41-64.

Sarkar, S. (2004a), Air Pollution: its Perilous Chronic Hygienic Impacts, *J. Hum. Ecol.,* 16(2): 129-132.

Sarkar, S. (2004b), *Extending Social Security Coverage to the Informal Sector in India, Social Change,* 34 (4): 122-130.

Sarkar, S. (2004c), Theorising in Informal Sector: Concept and Context, *Social Action,* 54(40): 359-373.

Sarkar, S. (2005), Economic Valuation and Health Linkages to Air Pollution, *International Journal of Environment and Development,* 2(2): 141-151.

Smith, K.R. (1987), *Biofuels, Air Pollution and Health: A Global Review,* Plenum Press, New York.

World Bank (1996), *Rural Energy and Development: Improving Energy Supplies to two Billion People,* Washington, DC.

Chapter - 9

Poverty and Sustainable Livelihood

INTRODUCTION

The concept of sustainable livelihoods is increasingly central to the debate about gender-development, poverty reduction and natural resource management. At an incredibly fundamental level, sustainable livelihoods are relating to the ways in which individuals and collectivities of individuals, make use of resources in order to survive. A resource at this point implies goods or services which individuals use to follow and preferably persuade their needs. Resources can be categorized into two general categories namely, natural and social. Natural resources are the physical inputs, which generate value and productivity in people's lives. Social resources are the social institutions and relationships that facilitate this process. Capital and resources are productive in the sense that they both facilitate ends, which would not be attainable in their absence (Coleman 1990). Like resources, capital can generate value and productivity for those who have it at their disposal. Its value, however, is defined in terms of its potential. Capital can be accumulated and transferred, but once it is used for a specific purpose, it becomes a resource. Social and natural capital then signify stocks of relationships and physical inputs which, when exploited, become resources. Along with social and natural capital, there are two other important categories like human and economic capital. Human capital refers to the skills, knowledge and intelligence that an individual holds at any point in his or her lifetime. Skills and knowledge can be built upon by broadening one's social relationships or investing economic capital or reinvesting human capital. They can also be depleted with disuse and with overuse. To the extent that it facilitates the acquisition of skills and knowledge, however, it can play an important role in developing human capital. Economic capital refers to the sum total of all of one's material possessions and investments, which can be converted into economic resources. One can use economic capital to acquire other forms of capital, including human capital, social capital and natural capital. Likewise, one can use human capital to acquire economic, social and natural capital and so on.

In an epoch of global social crisis characterized by increasing unemployment, jobless growth, and ecological destruction, a broader vision is needed to examine how people can meet their needs in a sustainable way. Attempting to solve the global employment crisis using conventional job creation through sustained economic growth cannot work. The concept of livelihood defined as means of living or of supporting life and meeting individual and community needs-provides new perspectives on developing healthy sustainable societies that provide people with secure and satisfying livelihoods. Sustainable livelihoods have been defined as people's capacities to generate and maintain their means of living, enhance their well being and that of future generations. These capacities are contingent upon the availability of and accessibility to options which are ecological, socio-cultural, economic and political and are predicated on equity, ownership of resources and participatory decision-making (Singh and Titi, 1994).

Sustainable livelihoods provide meaningful work that fulfills the social, economic, cultural, spiritual and ecological needs of all members of a community-human, non-human, present and future and safeguard cultural and biological diversity. The following is not an exhaustive listing of the components of sustainable livelihoods but an attempt to identify the key determinants.

- Promote equity between and among generations, races, genders and ethnic groups;
- Nurture a sense of place and connection to the local community, and adapt to and restore regional ecosystem;
- Stimulate local investment and help to keep capital within the local communities;
- Base production on renewable energy and on regenerating local resource endowments while reducing intensity of energy use eliminating over consumption of local and global resources and assuring no net loss of biodiversity;
- Utilize appropriate technology that is ecologically appropriate, socially just and humane, and that enhances rather than displaces community knowledge and skills;
- Strengthen the social economy and value non-monetary work as well as paid work;
- Provide secure access to opportunity and meaningful activity for all in community life.

These principles encompass a holistic set of values that are non-exploitative, promote participation in decision-making, emphasize the quality and creative nature of work, place needs over wants and foster healthy, mutually beneficial relationships among people and between people and their environment. It is hoped that these principles and their underlying values can stimulate further discussion. Sustainable livelihoods are supported by political, economic and social policies that enable mutually beneficial relationships to develop among people and the whole community of life. Economic globalization, on the other hand, primarily advances supernatural corporate interest, and is often inimical to human and environmental well being. Current policies externalize social and environmental costs, destroy ecosystems, pit localities into competition with one another and lower standards. Current measures ignore many of the crucial social functions on which all economies depend, in particular women's tremendous productive and reproductive roles. Policies are now geared toward economic growth based on over-consumption by the few while the needs of the many go unmet. Instead, socio-economic security and equity, meeting the needs of all and promoting authentic human development should be the overall goals of policy formulation. Policy formulation should begin by visioning processes that involve all sectors of community, as decisions made by all stakeholders better ensure equity, human rights and effective implementation. Central to a broad policy framework that supports sustainable livelihoods includes an investment in people and the environment as well as in physical capital, explicit recognition that women's empowerment is central to the achievement of broad-based socio-economic goals, broad public participation in the establishment of research priorities and the assessment and selection of technologies consistent with needs of sustainable communities and new resource accounting and institutional mechanisms for resource allocation and debt management and relief. Sustainable livelihoods require public participation and involvement in policy making at all levels to keep government agencies and officials responsive and accountable for their decisions and actions. Political reforms should both limit and make transparent the influence of corporate lobbies and campaign contributions. Corporations should be held accountable to a code of conduct based on principles of social and environmental responsibility. Multilateral trade agreements, treaties and conventions should not supersede local, state, and national sovereignty. Subsidiary should be an organizing principle of government, supporting the local rooted ness of livelihoods. To promote sustainable livelihoods, power must be rooted in the localized economies. Economic policy should be based on full-cost accounting, which incorporates social and environmental costs and benefits. Trade agreements and tax policies should favour local need over export marketing, encourage sustainable production and consumption and support renewable resource technologies. Such policies will support worker rights, debt relief and local control over resources within a framework of broader responsibility to share and protect resources. Socio-cultural policies should support principles of sustainable livelihoods in education, health, drawing on the wealth of cultural diversity and encouraging exchange of indigenous and modern knowledge, wisdom and skills. Special attention must be given to transforming structures that perpetuate inequity, injustice and intolerance, including those that perpetuate inequality and injustice toward women.

SUSTAINABLE APPROACHES TO POVERTY ALLEVIATION

The term sustainable livelihoods have been used to describe the integration of poverty reducing strategies, sustainable development, participation and empowerment processes into a framework for policy and project analysis and planning. (Loubser 1996). The millennium development goals have served to refocus the attention of the world community by setting ambitious targets for the elimination of poverty, while reaffirming the importance of ensuring environmental alongside social and economic sustainability, as the third pillar of sustainable development. The indicators used, however, to measure progress on the environment capture only a small proportion of the many real ways in which the livelihoods of the rural and urban poor depend on sustainable management of natural resources. As a consequence, it appears that insufficient attention is being paid to the environmental underpinnings of sustainable development.

governments need to adopt natural resource valuation and other methods that can help them to better assess the environmental sustainability of their development policies. No one questions the urgency of alleviating the suffering of people living in poverty. At the same time, there are large risks associated with short-term approaches to eradicating poverty, particularly where these rely on unsustainable use of natural resources and ecosystems. There is an urgent need to hark back of the real threat that ecosystem functions and species will be lost, and that the negative impact of such losses will fall largely on the poor. This is because poor people rely more heavily and more directly on local renewable resources for their livelihoods than other socioeconomic groups, and because the poor are more vulnerable to loss of environmental resources due to a lack of alternative assets. On the up side, the fact that many poor people live closely with natural resources and rely heavily on low input production systems give them an advantage in the development of new environmentally friendly products and services. From ecotourism schemes to organic agriculture, watershed protection contracts and carbon farming, there are a host of new livelihood opportunities where poor rural communities can compete without doing undue damage to their environment, provided they are not excluded by insecure land tenure, high transaction costs and other barriers to participation in emerging 'green' markets and the natural resources in question not destroyed through environmentally and socially perverse subsidies. At the same time, while the existence of win-win solutions such as 'green' markets is encouraging, we must not forget that in many cases there are significant trade-offs between environment and development objectives. In such cases there is an urgent need to improve the way in which human societies address environment/development trade-offs. Market-based mechanisms are part of the answer, but there is likewise a need for improved governance, to empower disenfranchised stakeholders to contribute to negotiated solutions, to ensure that the role of ecosystems as present and future livelihood support systems is taken into account in key public investment decisions, and to provide increased assistance from rich to poor countries to conserve ecosystems and prevent species extinctions.

The sustainable livelihoods approach can be seen as one of a number of analytical frameworks, which deal with the dynamic dimensions of poverty and well being through establishing a typology of assets which poor individuals; households and communities deploy to maintain well being under changing conditions. It has conceptual roots in various traditions, including applied social science, agro-eco systems/ farming systems analysis and especially participatory approaches to rural development. The main distinguishing feature of the approach is the attempt to set the analysis of livelihoods within a comprehensive framework, which encompasses policy and institutional processes at various levels, as well as micro level conditions, and determinants of livelihood. Some livelihoods approach for poverty removal has been the following:

- That poor people, especially in rural areas, manage a complex range of assets and activities to sustain themselves and that development professionals and officials often fail to adequately see and understand this. The approach has been the main corrective to the tendency for professionals to assume that everyone survives primarily by being within a household that has a limited number of economically active adults who are each engaged in one main job or occupation.
- That the poorest people are often disproportionately dependent on access to assets, which are not privately, owned common property or open access resources such as forests, common grazing land and fisheries.
- That effective poverty reduction through public budgets is not simply a question of what are classically perceived

as 'social expenditures' (health, education, welfare). Poor men and women also need access to a range of other assets and services, including financial services, markets, equitable justice systems. The key claims for the operational value of the sustainable livelihood approach are that it can promote: systematic analysis of poverty and its causes in a way that is holistic, realistic and manageable; a wider and better informed view of the opportunities for development activities and their likely impact; placing people and the priorities they define firmly at the centre of analysis

Participatory approaches have a contribution to make at each stage and participatory assessment methods provide one set of approaches, which are compatible with an assets/ vulnerability approach, but other types of analysis and information will also be needed in this context. Therefore it has been appeared explicitly at what a sustainable livelihood approach might contribute to the poverty removal strategy. Participatory practice can contribute to the poverty removal strategy process in several ways and at each stage (McGee and Norton 2000).

PARTICIPATORY APPROACHES

Analytical or diagnostic work

- Participatory research or consultative exercises involving poor communities in analyzing the nature, causes and dynamics of poverty, what their priorities for public action are and which institutions they see as effective. Participatory research for poverty assessment usually involves intermediary actors (research institutes, NGOs, service ministry and local government personnel). Participants need to be selected to provide a representative picture of livelihood conditions of the poor. The exercise is primarily a consultative one, but arguably, the creation of relationships among the various actors affected by or engaged in the policy process is the most significant innovation of participatory poverty assessment.

- Participation of civil society actors in analytical and research processes on institutional frameworks and national and local government budgets to contribute to identifying strategies and setting priorities.

Formulation of the strategy

- Joint formulation between civil society and government: Formulation of the poverty removal strategy can involve civil society specialists and advocates representing diverse groups from among the poor, as well as government technocrats and independent analysts. There will probably be little opportunity for direct involvement of poor people or community-level actors at this stage, although their interests can be represented by their intermediaries.
- Donors' participation in formulation is likely, although not necessarily desirable.

Approval

- Parliamentary approval: Poverty removal strategy needs to be approved by formal political structures within the country, as well as being approved at the global level by the World Bank and International Monetary Fund to trigger debt relief and concessional loans. While under formulation, the poverty removal strategy must pass through legitimate democratic political processes and ultimately attain formal ratification by elected political representatives.
- Public approval: Given the stress placed on civil society engagement with the poverty removal strategy process, it is vital to the poverty removal strategy credibility and implementation that civil society itself holds a well-

publicized national dialogue around the poverty removal strategy process which culminates in its public endorsement of the final product.

- Donor agencies will need their Boards to approve programmes associated with the poverty removal strategy, but these approval processes do not need to proceed in step with the country process.

Implementation

- Negotiating roles, responsibilities and entitlements at the local level: The poverty removal strategy can only provide a framework for empowerment if people in poor communities are clear about what they can and cannot expect from public agencies, and can make claims according to their expectations. Thus the negotiation and communication of roles, responsibilities and entitlements relating to the poverty removal strategy are crucial. These local level negotiations will, of course, occur against a backdrop of all the normal structures of local development and government and must iterate with them rather than supplant or contradict them.
- Monitoring the effectiveness of policy measures: Participatory approaches can be used to test the effectiveness of policy changes by monitoring the changes actually experienced by local level actors, against the implementation of policy goals.
- Citizens' monitoring of outcomes: Citizens can be directly involved in formulating and monitoring local budget, and in monitoring service delivery, and holding service providers and local government to account.

Impact Assessment or Evaluation

- In addition to the monitoring of poverty removal strategy implementation, there may also be an attempt to evaluate the poverty removal strategy retrospectively and synthesize lessons from it to inform future policy. During poverty removal strategy evaluation, participatory approaches can contribute through gathering perceptions of the strengths and weaknesses of the poverty removal strategy experience from actors at multiple levels, including community, street-level bureaucrats, local government staff, civil society representatives, politicians and central government technocrats. The perceptions of these actors on the poverty removal strategy process, content and outcomes can be fed into formal processes for assessing policy change and impact.

SUSTAINABLE LIVELIHOOD APPROACH

Analytical or Diagnostic Work

Integrate household survey, environmental, social and political analysis to identify livelihood groups; identify trends, threats to existing livelihoods (supplementing expenditure/income analysis with information on trends in assets held by the poor, the returns obtained from them, the costs required to sustain them). Identify issues poor groups themselves prioritize.

Formulation of the Strategy

Integrate asset/vulnerability information with economic analysis, to identify which interventions have biggest sustainable impact on most poor people at affordable cost; and which interventions have most positive impact on identified poorest and most vulnerable groups. A sustainable livelihood approach could help to bring household expenditure/income data into a common frame with information on assets, including what is required to maintain and enhance them, and what returns might be. Participatory analysis might be used to identify how different groups may react to new conditions, threats, and opportunities. The vulnerability framework might be captured by modeling alternatives to traditional economic assumptions of income maximization, e.g. maximizing worst-case expenditure, or maximization subject to at least achieving a minimum expenditure level. In moving the sustainable livelihood framework from local to national concerns, some sacrifice of the detailed, holistic approach will be required, but the analysis can inform decisions on where the main variations lie, and what features are important.

Approval

By identifying the importance of heterogeneity, a sustainable livelihood approach might help promote a more decentralized and locally responsive approach, in which the centre is approving a process by which resources are allocated but with greater discretion for adaptation through local level planning and budgeting processes.

Implementation

The sustainable livelihood approach can inform the development of frameworks for setting objectives and designing monitoring systems, which capture early-warning indicators of poverty, including asset sales.

Impact Assessment

Recognition of need to assess longer term trends in assets, especially environmental assets.

LIVELIHOOD STRATEGIES FOR ENVIRONMENTAL SECURITY

The concept of environmental security provides a means for assessing and addressing threats in an increasingly interdependent and environmental degradation. Natural resource dependent individuals and communities become marginalized because they either have no rights to the resources on which they are dependent or no feasible way to exercise the rights they do have. Conflicts between traditional and contemporary systems of property rights are often at the root of livelihood and environmental insecurity. The most vulnerable communities are invariably the poorest and most marginalized, for whom alternatives are non-existent or come at exorbitant cost. The regions affected by these conditions are where environmental insecurity is most likely to lead to conflict.

Recent advances in understanding the causes of poverty, the sources of economic growth, and the measurement of human well being, have reemphasized the role of natural capital in human development. People, particularly rural poor, need secure access to productive ecosystems as well as the security of a healthy environment in order to create and sustain their livelihoods. The majority of the world's poor people continue to live in rural areas. The World Bank estimated recently that around 75 per cent of the world's poor people reside in rural space and that the rural poor will outnumber their urban counterparts for at least another generation. Rural people use many ecosystems as essential productive assets, whether on a day-to-day basis or seasonally. Farmers who cannot afford to buy fertilizer transfer soil fertility from woodlands to their fields, either directly through litter harvesting or through using manure from browsing livestock. In African dry land farming systems, where seasonal food shortages are common, dry-season flood plain grazing and fisheries, and the collection and sale of non-timber forest products provide a lifeline during times of need. Natural resources are thus a key element of the risk management strategies of the rural poor. Local communities should be recognized and empowered as legitimate and effective stewards of natural resources and ecosystem services. The importance of natural resources in directly supporting human livelihoods is often overlooked, as the goods and services they yield are either for subsistence purposes, or traded informally, so they do not show up in national economic statistics.

Governments need to apply the precautionary approach in decisions about the use and conversion of productive ecosystems. Goods and services provided by productive ecosystems are the cornerstone of the livelihoods of the rural poor, while also providing urban populations with a number of key services, such as clean water. Ecosystem conservation can also literally be a matter of life and death. Governments need to identify and safeguard ecosystems essential for preventing and mitigating the impact of natural disasters in collaboration with local communities. Paradoxically, it may well be easier to exhibit the value to local livelihoods of natural resources once they have been severely degraded. Where this has happened, for instance through ill-advised development schemes, the local people will be aware of what they lost. Also it will be easier to do robust valuation exercises on the basis of real data, and mobilize both political and local support for their application. Access to natural resources, often managed by local communities as common property, is a key livelihood asset for most of the rural poor and will continue to be so in the foreseeable future. Such assets enable the poor to manage risk by spreading production across a diverse portfolio of natural resources. But many common property resources are under increasing pressure from encroachment and destructive resource extraction by outsiders. This leads to loss of livelihoods, which in turn undermines social cohesion and stability, leading to increased poverty, social friction and political tension. In extreme cases, these tensions lead to violent conflict, which diverts vital development resources to meet urgent humanitarian and peacekeeping needs. Communities need to be empowered to manage the ecosystems they depend upon, and be protected from exploitation by powerful outsiders. Listening to communities' own perceptions of environment and development problems and solutions will be essential in order to integrate indigenous knowledge in solutions that are commensurate with their needs and aspirations.

Technological changes aimed at increasing income are unlikely to be adopted unless they are compatible with the risk management strategies of the rural poor. The productive ecosystems provide options for improving the livelihoods of future generations, whereas ecosystem depletion and species extinction reduce capacity to adapt to future stresses such as climate change, and respond to opportunities such as the marketing of ecological services.

It had already been recognized that, although watershed development can contribute to enhance livelihoods for a growing rural population, it is not a panacea (Turton and Farrington 1998). A key consequence of broadening out the sectoral contribution to poverty elimination is the need to base water supply activities on an analysis of water-livelihoods linkages. This demands better quality socio-economic data on time expenditure, relative costs of time for other activities, patterns of labour demand within households, intra-household decision making on the division of labour (who benefits, who loses), what the increasing availability of water at a household level means in terms of priority usage and how this translates into income, health, education and other benefits. A livelihoods approach involves, therefore, a broader approach than simply seeking epidemiological improvements. It challenges the regular integration of water supply, sanitation and hygiene education. The decision as to where and when to combine water supply with sanitation and hygiene education should be based on an assessment of the relative costs and benefits in particular contexts of undertaking one or all of the interventions. The sustainable livelihood approach provides a framework for analyzing the fit between watershed development activities, rural livelihoods and ultimately poverty reduction (Table 1).

Common pool resources represent a form of natural and social capital that individuals and communities can draw on in pursuit of their livelihood strategies. They form a part of rural peoples' strategies for adjusting to the harsh and stressful environment. The role of common pool resource is particularly important in lean times, acting as a buffer in times of drought or other crises. During droughts, the collection of tubers and wild foods from the forest is an important coping mechanism. It also provides independent sources of income to women, through, for instance, goat rearing, broom making, leaf plate making and collection of tendu leaves and tamarind (Lokur-Pangare 1998). All of these occupations depend upon common pool resource, either for fodder or raw materials. The key question is the extent to which the poor retain access to common pool resource after watershed development efforts have taken place.

Table 1
Sustainable Livelihoods and Watershed Development

Livelihood	Key Issues
Component Capital Assets	Which assets are most important to the poor? Are there particular combinations of capital assets or sequences in their development, which increase the likelihood that watershed development will succeed? Has access by the poor to common property improved as a result of watershed development?
Livelihood Strategies	Does watershed development support the livelihood strategies of the poor?How does watershed development interface with other livelihood strategies?How do people's livelihood strategies affect their participation in and benefit from watershed development?
Sustainable Livelihood Outcomes	What contribution has watershed development made to sustainable livelihoods?What are the relevant outcome indicators?Are people's own livelihood priorities being addressed?How can activities be adapted in order to enhance livelihood impacts on target groups, while remaining consistent with the overall objectives?

Source: Turton [2000].

Within the forest sector, key constraints to improving forest-based livelihoods lie in the institutional environment and in particular in the relationships between and within the forest department, the forest users and the enabling environment (Hobley and Shields 2000). The issues surrounding non-timber forest product management are used as an example to show the importance of understanding the linkages between forest product usage and livelihood security. Non-timber forest product is an important element of poorer households livelihood systems through food security and employment. It also provides an important part of the family income throughout the year, especially in poorer communities. Depending on other employment opportunities, non-timber forest product can provide an economic activity to fill seasonal gaps in other work or become the activity of choice during the season for collection of high value non-timber forest product. Poor forest dwellers and landless or marginal farmers are the most dependent on non-timber forest product for their livelihoods. Having such an important stake in the forest, they have the most to gain from better protection of non-timber forest product and forest resources. These are the groups with the strongest potential reasons for protecting the resource, given sufficient support and incentives. This rationale formed the basis for testing of new management and marketing arrangements for non-timber forest product based on the principles of participatory forest management planning. These systems are still under development and review but they do provide the opportunity for significant change in livelihood security for a group of poor forest-dependent households, illustrating the importance of understanding the institutional framework and the power relations between different groups in order to effect change in access to livelihood assets.

Poor households often adopt strategy to accommodate the impact of increased direct and indirect energy costs by switching over to cheaper options. This has involved a shift down the energy ladder. The several researches show that energy is significant for the livelihoods of the poor (Sarkar 2005; World Bank 2000). Poor households adopted three main strategies to accommodate these energy changes namely, switching to cheaper energy options; reducing the overall consumption of energy and reducing their expenditure on non-energy goods. The energy changes which households had to accommodate had a dismal effect on their assets and resulted in increased vulnerability for all the poor households. The sustainable livelihood framework was a very useful instrument for unpacking the macro-meso-micro energy linkages. It was possible, using the sustainable livelihoods framework to unpack the link between changes in macro policies and livelihoods, showing that all the livelihoods of the study households became more vulnerable as a result of policy changes. The sustainable livelihood framework was a valuable and robust analytical tool for unpacking the energy-poverty relationship. It provides a set of elements against which to systematically assess the impact of contextual variables; as well as policies, institutions and processes on the livelihoods of poor urban households. It was a useful tool for demonstrating the impact of policies, institutions, and processes on poor households. Furthermore, the sustainable livelihood framework provided a valuable structure for aiding discourse and understanding between energy and social development poverty focused stakeholders at government and community levels. The poverty and development experts became increasingly responsive of the importance that poor households placed on access to energy.

CONCLUDING REMARKS

There are many ways of applying sustainable livelihood approaches. The livelihoods approaches may be of putting livelihoods as the focus and enhancing livelihood impacts as a central aim in making recommendations or exploring livelihood priorities of local people and how they are affected by natural resources management interventions. Livelihoods analysis can be put to a variety of uses. It is not only a tool for project design but can be used for reshaping a sectoral or programme intervention for better fit with livelihoods, impact assessment of a project/programme, understanding factors affecting local participation in an initiative and participatory planning with communities. It can be very useful for a review or 'standing back' from a programme, even if it was not designed explicitly with livelihood objectives. Livelihoods analysis can be done without the sustainable livelihood framework, but the framework is helpful in broadening and structuring the scope of enquiry. However, elements that is not explicit in the framework need to be brought up-front. It is very difficult to say how much livelihood security or sustainability has changed. Livelihoods analysis is more likely to show how livelihoods are being supported or constrained. This is useful for generating recommendations on how to enhance the 'fit' between a new initiative and people's livelihood priorities or address a conflict between them. But it is less useful for aggregating results and providing succinct punchy findings to policymakers.

Sustainable poverty elimination will be achieved only if external support focuses on what matters to people, understands the differences between groups of people and works with them in a way that is congruent with their current livelihood strategies, social environment and ability to adapt. Poverty elimination is an enormous challenge that will only be overcome by working at multiple levels, ensuring that micro level activity informs the development of policy and an effective enabling environment and those macro level structures and processes support people to build on their strengths. Linking micro and the macro levels in the livelihoods framework demands that policy and institutional analysis must take place at all levels and include gender analysis.

Access to natural resources, often managed by local communities as common property, is a key livelihood asset for most of the rural poor and will continue to be so in the foreseeable future. Such assets enable the poor to manage risk by spreading production across a diverse portfolio of natural resources. But many common property resources are under increasing pressure from encroachment and destructive resource extraction by outsiders. This leads to loss of livelihoods, which in turn undermines social cohesion and stability, leading to increased poverty, social friction and political tension. In extreme cases, these tensions lead to violent conflict, which diverts vital development resources to meet urgent humanitarian and peacekeeping needs. Communities need to be empowered to manage the ecosystems they depend upon and be protected from exploitation by powerful outsiders. Listening to communities' own perceptions of environment and development problems and solutions will be essential in order to integrate indigenous knowledge in solutions that are commensurate with their needs and aspirations.

REFERENCES

Coleman, James S. (1990), *Foundations of Social Theory,* Belknap Press of Harvard University, London.

Loubser, J. (1996), *Sustainable Livelihoods: A Conceptual Exploration*, Report of 1994-95 SID/PIED Workshops on Civil Society and Sustainable Livelihoods held in Asia, sub-Saharan Africa, Latin America and North America, Society for International Development and Center for Respect of Life and Environment, Rome.

Hobley, M. and Shields, D. (2000), *The Reality of Trying to Transform Structures and Processes: Forestry in Rural Livelihoods*, ODI Working Paper 132, Overseas Development Institute, London.

Lokur-Pangare, V. (1998), *Gender issues in Watershed Development and Management in India*, Agricultural Research and Extension Network Paper 38, Overseas Development Institute, London.

McGee, R. and Norton, A. (2000), *Participation in Poverty Reduction Strategies: A Synthesis of Experience with Participatory Approaches to Policy Design, Implementation and Monitoring,* IDS Working Paper 109, Institute of Development Studies, Brighton.

Norton, A. and Foster, M. (2001), *The Potential of Using Sustainable Livelihoods Approaches in Poverty Reduction Strategy Papers,* Working Paper 148, Overseas Development Institute, London.

Sarkar, S. (2005), Economic Valuation and Health Linkages to Indoor Air Pollution, *International Journal of Environment and Development*, 2 (2): 141-151.

Singh, N. and Titi, V. (1994), *Adaptive Strategies of the Poor in Arid and Semi-Arid Lands: In Search of Sustainable Livelihoods*, International Institute for Sustainable Development, Winnipeg.

Turton, C. and Farrington, J. (1998), *Enhancing Rural Livelihoods through Participatory Watershed Development in India,* Natural Resources Perspectives 34, Overseas Development Institute, London.

Turton, C. (2000), *Enhancing Livelihoods through Participatory Watershed Development in India*, ODI Working Paper 131, Overseas Development Institute, London.

World Bank (2000), *Household Energy, Air Pollution and Health,* UNDP/ESMAP.

Chapter - 10

Work Rights and Occupational Health

INTRODUCTION

Since women work is largely and still is in many developing countries carried out in the household and informal sector, it has been scrutinized as non-productive and thus often debarred from economic activities (Sarkar 2005a). As a result, domestic work and work based in homes bring about no direct payments, no protective legislation, no socio-economic security and stumpy social status. Women and men usually carry out different tasks and work in different sectors. Women are more likely to work in the informal sector and work from their homes (World Health Organization 2004).

In India the informal sector employs more than 90 per cent of workforce, most if not all, are covered by meaningful social security schemes. The informalised workforce is unprotected labour, which implies labour that does not have any socio-economic safety. The protection that a society provides to individuals and households to ensure access to wage and working conditions in a comprehensive sense, in matters of security of employment, health care, maternity benefits, provident fund, retirement benefits, is an essential element of the safety nets that keeps working people and their families from falling into poverty (Sarkar 2004).

The informal sector represents an important part of the economy and certainly of labour market in many countries, especially developing countries and poses a challenge to policy makers with regard to issues relating to improvement of the working condition and social protection of the workers engaged in the informal sector. In the developing economies a substantial share of employment is indeed in informal category and women in all age groups depend on the informal sector more heavily than men. Women and children are over represented in this sector in the sense that their share in the sector is higher than their share in total labour force. Most women tend to be own account workers and only a few are heads of micro enterprises. Relatively lower level of education among women, compared to men, seems to explain, in part, this gender differential in informal employment. Discrimination in the labour market also explains in part the disproportionate concentration as it limits women's access to formal and wage employment. Women also face additional constraints because of their homemaking and childcare responsibilities, which limit their participation in formal employment. Even within the informal sector more women than men seem to be in poor quality employment.

Homemakers are not explicitly regarded as workers, homes are not regarded as workplaces and household labour is not considered as work. Despite these biases the rising visibility and magnitude of women's labour can no longer be ignored and neglected in policy and research. Highly gendered labour has overriding significance in relation to the hierarchical ordering in terms of wealth and status. One's occupation and the position it provides, is strongly associated with differences in life chances, freedoms, opportunities and living conditions, and thereby also significantly influences the possibility of sound health. Therefore, the interface between gender and work is a key issue within discussions of social inequalities in general and gender inequalities in health in particular. Women in general relative to men face unequal hiring standards, unequal opportunities for training, unequal pay for equal work, unequal access to productive resources, segregation and concentration in female sectors and occupations, different physical and mental working conditions, unequal participation in economic decision-making and unequal promotion prospects. These factors negatively affect women's social status and their position in society relative to men, and consequently have an impact on gender inequalities in health.

In high-income, advanced countries, despite women's poorer position and discrimination in most sectors and levels of working life, their amplified participation in gainful employment has not only strengthened women's social status and their individual and family's economic situation, but has also been beneficial to their physical condition (Waldron *et al.* 1998). Employment outside the home is an important source of social support and self-esteem, which helps women to be integrated into society and to avoid social isolation in the home. Studies have shown that working outside the home is associated with better mental and physical health of women. Income from work outside the home may also reduce women's economic and social dependence on their male partner. In general, a positive relationship has been found in a number of studies between multiple roles and health through the pathway of self-confidence and economic independence. These positive pathways may outweigh the additional stress that comes from the responsibilities of several positions. These results may also hold for women from middle or upper income households in poorer countries, but we have little actual data to support this.

This general observation obtained mainly from research in high-income countries may, however, not always apply to women in low-income countries where large numbers are exposed to harmful working environments and often have few choices about whether and where to work. The latter is also often true in higher income countries especially for poorer women. There is little evidence in these circumstances to suggest that women who work outside the home are better off. For these reasons, women working outside the home are often seen as a negative status symbol by the family denoting its low economic and social status. In South Asia, for example, while women from the poorest households often work outside the home, households are known to 'withdraw' women from such work once their economic status improves. Nonetheless, even in such situations, poor women who work outside the home evidence greater levels of self-confidence and economic independence, even though they may face hazardous working conditions, stress, and violence (Razavi *et al.* 2000). There is a huge body of occupational health literature showing how work creates exposures to numerous risks and hazards that, regardless of being paid or unpaid, can impair health. These hazards are related to both physical and psychosocial exposures at work. The quantity of health damaging factors varies tremendously between different occupations and across countries, as well as between formal and informal sector jobs. Adverse health effects at work may result in absences due to sickness, early retirement or unemployment, which in turn may lead to curve down in household incomes, especially in countries with inadequate or effective social safety nets.

GENDER DIVISION OF LABOUR

Gender division of work is an imperative basis for identifying risks in the work environments for women and men and understanding gender inequalities in work-related mortality and morbidity. Working and employment conditions may differ by sex. In some countries, women lift heavy loads and men do most administrative work, while in others the opposite situation exists. In one country, women are more likely to be unemployed but in others, men are more often without jobs. Women tend to work more hours at home and fewer outside of the home, and they usually take primary responsibility for family well being. The gender division of labour is just as obvious within the family and household as within waged employment in both formal and informal sectors. In the field of the household, gender segregation of work usually means, that the main part of the household responsibilities including daily tasks of cooking, cleaning the house, doing the laundry and caring for children and sick relatives are allocated to women, whereas daily and household maintenance are men's responsibility. One important characteristic of women's work in the household is that it cannot be postponed, and as a result women's leisure time is more fragmented than that of men (Frankenhaeuser *et al.* 1991).

Gender segregation of labour in both paid and unpaid work may be linked to gender inequities in health in at least two ways. First, gender inequities in occupational health may occur if women are working in intrinsically more unhealthy jobs and/or if certain jobs remain unhealthy because these are female-dominated. One finds support for both explanations in the scientific literature. Evidence suggests that women's unhealthy working conditions and occupational health problems are less likely to be addressed by employers, unions, researchers and policy makers, which further contribute to gender inequities in occupational health. Their focus has traditionally been directed towards health hazards in male-dominated working environments. Male-dominated workplaces are still considered more dangerous in terms of for example risk of fatal accidents and chemical health hazards than female dominated work environments. As a result, men's jobs are also better paid than women's jobs. In addition, resources allocated for research and policies to improve the working conditions of men have been more substantial compared with resources allocated for female-dominated work settings.

HEALTH RISK

It is important to note that even if women are exposed to a particular health-damaging factor to the same degree as men, they may experience worse health effects due to both biological and social factors. Furthermore since neither women nor men are homogenous categories, a large variations regarding health damaging working conditions across different groups of women and different groups of men has been identified. This lack of visibility is even more problematic from a gender perspective as women are more prone to work related injuries at home, whereas men more often than women suffer from occupational accidents outside the home.

There is little data on women in low-income countries, but they are known to shoulder extremely heavy physical workloads, both at home and at work. Women provide water and fuel, carrying heavy loads and walking long distances. These constraints can lead to musculoskeletal disorders and reproductive problems. Washing and cooking expose women to water-related diseases such as schistosomiasis, malaria and worms. Women cooking on open stoves risk burns and exposure to smoke containing toxic pollutants. Smoke and fumes resulting from indoor use of biofuels jeopardize health standards more than any other outdoor degradation. In India the most important disease associated with indoor and outdoor air pollution is probably acute respiratory infection (Sarkar 2005b). Women cooking with open stoves have greater risks of illness due to smoke pollution. Women's respiratory disorders in India were found to be linked to domestic exposure to cooking smoke.

The risks of mental ill health among full-time homemakers should not be underestimated. The housewives are more affected by psychological distress than employed women, probably as a result of isolation in the home. Housewives have more sick-days, more limitations in activity, more acute and chronic conditions, less favourable levels of serum cholesterol and lipoproteins, and higher risk of coronary heart disease (Hall 1990). For women in paid employment, sexual harassment at work place is common and may result in guilt, shame, anxiety, depression and other health consequences.

In a large number of low-income countries many opportunities for women to earn income exist in the field of agriculture. The women spend long hours in uncomfortable working postures, which can lead to chronic leg and back pain amongst other. Besides the health risks that are present in subsistence agricultural work, cash crop production of, for example fruits, vegetables and flowers involves in addition exposure to toxic pesticides. In the low-income countries many women are facing problems of working in chemical laced water when transplanting rice. Because of the gender division of labour, women are more involved than men in hand labour, such as weeding, picking and sorting in the fields that have been sprayed, which results in prolonged exposure to pesticides. Men, on the other hand, are more involved in fumigating crops, which entails exposure for short periods of time. As a result, the extensive use of pesticides constitutes a major health risk for women, and one that is greater for women than for men.

A large body of literature indicates that employment is beneficial for men's health and survival. However, men have many more occupational accidents than women, and more fatal injuries in all jurisdictions where data are available. In addition, men in the developed countries report more exposure than women to noise, vibrations, extreme temperatures, chemicals and lifting heavy weights. Many societies accept the idea that men can be asked to do more hazardous jobs, although in others, men resist if they feel they are asked to do harder jobs. In still others, it is taken for granted that women will do most heavy lifting and carrying (World Health Organization 2004).

CONCLUDING REMARKS

Women's escalating participation in the market economy has challenged the view of gender socially and culturally determined roles and responsibilities. Occupational health research, that traditionally has conceptualized work as paid work undertaken by men, and accordingly focused on occupational health risks in male dominated occupations, can no longer be justified. However, efforts to include women in occupational health studies by trying to understand women's work-related health using solely a structural framework for paid employment also proved not to be adequate. Women's work-related health cannot be understood without complementing the framework based on waged employment with other frameworks related to gender roles and women's work in the domestic sphere. Both women and men are facing different risks due to the gender division of labour or they are exposed to the same risks in different degree. When women and men are exposed equally to the same risk factor, they may not suffer the same health consequences because of biological and social reasons. Policy analysis should also take into account gender differences in precarious and non-standard employment. Specific health risks are associated with specific types of precarious or contingent work. Home based work presents very different challenges from those presented by work for temporary or part-time work. Policy applicable to specific types of contingent work should be scrutinized with regard to gendered effects (World Health Organization 2004). Working life is one of the most important arenas for action to improve the health status of populations and to reduce gender inequality in health.

Working life is one of the most important arenas for action to improve the health status of populations and to reduce gender inequality in health. New approaches and strategies are needed that would encourage stakeholders to enforce health and safety regulations in the informal economy. Occupational health standards should be reviewed through a gender lens and examined for systemic discrimination and adjustments should be made based on the results. However, careful attention should be paid so that such adjustments do not paradoxically reinforce occupational segregation and discrimination. Strengthening of support services for occupational health is needed, especially for workers in the informal sector and in precarious work. Men and women workers should be given a more active role in developing policies to promote healthier workplaces. Women and men should be treated equally at work. They should be hired at all levels of the occupational health prevention and compensation systems. Because low wages are an increasingly important contributor to poverty, women and men should receive equal pay for work of equal value.

REFERENCES

Frankenhaeuser, M. *et al.* (1991), *Women, Work and Health: Stress and Opportunities,* Plenum Press, New York.

Hall, E.M. (1990), *Women's Work: An Inquiry into the Health Effects of Invisible and Visible Labour,* Karolinska Institute, Stockholm.

Razavi, S. *et al.* (2000), *Gendered Poverty and Well Being,* Blackwell Publishers, Oxford.

Sarkar, S.(2004), Extending Social Security Coverage to the Informal Sector in India, *Social Change*, 34 (4): 122-130.

Sarkar, S.(2005a),The Conceptual and Theoretical Framework of Informal Sector: A Review of Literature in Developed and Developing Countries, *Journal of Social and Economic Policy*, 2 (2): 187-205.

Sarkar, S. (2005b), Natural Resource Environment, Pollution and Women Health, In: T. Sabanna (ed.), *WTO and the Agriculture,* Serials Publications, New Delhi.

Waldron, I. *et al.*(1998), Interacting Effects of Multiple Roles on Women's Health, *Journal of Health and Social Behaviour*, 39: 216-236.

World Health Organization (2004), *Gender, Health and Work,* Geneva.

Index